MIDDLE ENGLISH READINGS

IN

TRANSLATION

Middle English Readings in Translation

By

FRANCIS X. CORRIGAN
Pace College, New York

THE CHRISTOPHER PUBLISHING HOUSE
BOSTON, U.S.A.

TABLE OF CONTENTS

PREFACE

This book was prepared with the specific wish that it will be most helpful to college and university students working in the field of Middle English literature and, more especially, studying the history of the English language of this particular period.

While many of these selections have little or no literary value as such, indubitably many others do; nevertheless, all of them together do give the student a true, vivid, representative, and rather wide view of the religious, political, and social ideas, beliefs, hopes, fears, and interests that certainly occupied the minds and motivated the wills, in varying degrees, of all the people in Medieval Europe and particularly Medieval England.

However, more to the point. The true worth of these translations lies in their linguistic value, for special care was taken, in the faithful and thoughtful execution of each word, to render it into Modern English, exactly as it was used in Middle English, the only exception being the elimination of the prolific use of the unneeded, as far as we are concerned today, double and treble negatives appearing in the same sentence. Of course, it is no secret that the practice of using double and treble negatives in a sentence is still very much in evidence and use but only, we like to believe, reluctantly, among the Americans and Englishmen who speak a substandard level of English but who are actually the true heirs and makers of the historical language. Yet, notwithstanding all this, students know from their high school and college English classes that such a usage is now more than frowned upon in standard speech, oral and written.

In this work, too, diligent attention was paid to the accurate use of the tense and form of the verb, to the proper number of the noun, and to the proper number and person of the pronoun. Wherever an addition of a word or words was needed to clarify a passage, such additions were made and are placed in brackets; also, in most instances, where the Middle English has the combination of a plural subject with a singular verb or vice-versa, this translation follows the original use. Incidentally, I made no effort to reproduce the rime or rhythm found in the Middle English poetic selections, and wherever such, the rime and the rhythm, do occasionally occur, it is purely accidental on my part.

In bringing this work to a happy fruition, I wish to acknowledge my debt to my family, to the late Professor John F. X. O'Neill, Ph.D., who first led me into the study of English philology over twenty years ago, and to Professor Oliver F. Emerson, Ph.D., whose helpful and scholarly books I have used through the years.

Flushing, 1963   *F. X. C.*

MIDDLE ENGLISH READINGS
IN
TRANSLATION

INTRODUCTION

In the Middle English period (1100-1500), there were a tremendous number of dialects spoken throughout England, and these spoken dialects differed substantially in some ways from county to county. In some places, there were even dialectal differences within the same county. Yet, for all this linguistic confusion, more apparent than real, it seems to me, three major dialects, based on geographical location, were fairly well recognizable, namely:

1. Northern, the dialect used north of the Humber River,
2. Southern, the dialect used south of the Thames River, and
3. Midland, the dialect used in the area between the Humber and the Thames.

Ranulphus Higden of Chester wrote his *Polychronicon* in Latin and told, in his own way, the history of the world up to the year 1342. Then John Trevisa, a canon at Westbury, in Gloucestershire, translated Higden's work into English, adding material of his own and bringing the account up to 1387, the year he finished his book. About the differences of two of the major dialects, Northern and Southern, Trevisa wrote, "All the language of the Northumbrians [the Northern dialect] and especially at York, is so sharp, slittering, and harsh sounding and unpleasant that we southern men scarcely understand the language."

Even as late as the end of the fifteenth century, this problem of dialect was still present, for the printer, William

Caxton (1421?-1491), who used London English himself, was not certain what form of the language he should use in his works. In the prologue of his version of the *Aeneid,* he shows his concern:

> And certainly our language now used varyeth far from that which was used and spoken when I was born. For we Englishmen be born under the domination of the moon, which is never steadfast but ever wavering, waxing one season and waneth and decreaseth another season. And that common English that is spoken in one shire varyeth from another. Insomuch that in my days happened that certain merchants were in a ship in Thames, for to have sailed over the sea into Zeeland, and for lack of wind they tarried at the Foreland and went on land for to refresh them. And one of them, named Sheffield, a mercer, came into a house and axed for meat, and specially he axed after eggs; and the good wife answered that she could speak no French. And the merchant was angry for he also could speak no French, but would have had eggs and she understood him not. And then at last another said that he would have eiren, then the good wife said that she understood him well. Lo, what should a man in these days now write, *eggs* or *eiren.* Certainly it is hard to please every man because of the diversity and change of language.

O. F. Emerson, in his book, *The History of the English Language,* states that the first clear recognition of the fact that London English was the standard written language did not occur until 1589, when the *Art of English Poesie,* attributed to George Puttenham, was published. Puttenham's advice to the poet in the use of language is of special interest, also:

Our maker [the poet], therefore, at these days shall not . . . take the terms [words and idioms] of Northern men, such as they use in daily talk, whether they be noblemen or gentlemen, or of their best clerks all is a matter; nor in effect any speech used beyond the river Trent, though no man can deny but that theirs is the purer English Saxon at this day. Yet, it is not so courtly nor so current as our Southern English is, no more is the far Western man's speech. Ye shall therefore take the usual speech of the court, and that of London and the shires lying about London within sixty miles, and not much above. I say not this, but in every shire of England there be gentlemen and others that speak, but especially write as good Southern as we of Middlesex or Surrey do, but not the common people of every shire, to whom the gentlemen and also the learned clerks do for the most part condescend; but herein we are already ruled by the English dictionaries and other books written by learned men, and therefore it needeth none other direction in that behalf.

While the above quotation does show a conscious awareness of the emerging importance of London English, the statement can also mislead the student on two points. When Puttenham says, "write as good Southern as we of Middlesex or Surrey do," the student should not think that he is talking about the Southern dialect, because he is referring to the Midland dialect, London English, specifically, Southeast Midland. The second point is another matter. Of course, we do not know everything about all these events even today, but we do know that when he wrote that the men of his day "are ruled already by the English dictionaries," he certainly was not thinking of dictionaries as we know them, for the first English dictionary, called *The Table Alphabeticall of Hard Words,* was written by Robert Cawdrey and published in 1604, fifteen years after the appearance of the *Art of English Poesie.*

In the very readable but scholarly volume, *The History of the English Language,** Professor Albert C. Baugh states that the history of Standard English is for all practical purposes the history of London English. But what are the reasons for this pre-eminent emergence of London English over all the other dialects? Generally, three factors are recognized for this phenomenon, namely; London is the capital city, the Universities of Cambridge and Oxford are located nearby, and Geoffrey Chaucer wrote his *Canterbury Tales* in this dialect. Many authorities dispute the influence of Chaucer in this matter, claiming that he wrote in this dialect, because even in the fourteenth century it was quite evident that this dialect was assuming national importance and because it was the dialect of his place of birth, of his boyhood, of his manhood, and even of his old age. However, there is no one around who claims he ever hindered this development! The part that Oxford played is debatable, for its dialect was as much Southern as Midland. The simple reason for the emergence of the London dialect and indeed for the emergence of London itself as the capital city, I believe, must be attributed to, as Trevisa says in his translation, "better corn land, more people, more noble cities, and more profitable harbors," for it seems to be a law of nature that culture grows in rich soil, or to put it another way, culture follows wealth and power. The court, of course, is another factor, but I can not imagine the court being anywhere but where the wealth and power would be.

---

* Copyright © 1935 by D. Appleton-Century Company, Inc., and copyright © 1957 by Appleton-Century-Crofts, Inc.

Middle English Readings in Translation

THE PETERBOROUGH CHRONICLE

1132. In this year, King Henry came to this land. Then came Henry the abbot and betrayed the monks of the Borough to the king, because he [the abbot] wished to subject that monastery to Cluny so that the king was well nigh deceived and sent after the monks. And through the mercy of God and through the Bishop of Salisbury and the Bishop of Lincoln and the other powerful men who were there, the king then knew that he [the abbot] acted with deceit. When he might no longer [deceive the king], then he desired that his nephew should become the abbot in the Borough, but Christ willed it not. It was not very long thereafter, that the king sent after him and made him give up that office of the abbot in the Borough and go out of the land; and the king gave that abbacy to the Prior of Saint Neot's, Martin was [he] called. He came on St. Peter's massday with much solemnity into the monastery.

1135. In this year, the king went over the sea at Lammas. And the second day that he lay asleep in the ship, then the day became dark all over the land and the sun became as it were a three night old moon and the stars [were] about it at midday. Men became startled and frightened and said that many things should come hereafter, as did; because in that same year, the king died the second day after St. Andrew's massday in Normandy. Then treason was in the land, for every man soon robbed the other whom [he]

15

might. Then his son and his friends took and brought his body to England and buried [him] at Reading. A good man was he and [there] was much fear of him. No man dared harm another in his time. Peace he made for men and animals. Whosoever bore his burden, gold or silver, no man dared say anything to him but good.

Meanwhile his nephew was come to England, Stephen of Blois, and came to London, and the people of London received him and sent after the Archbishop, William Curbeuil, and consecrated him king on midwinter's day. In this king's time, there was all discord and evil and robbery, because against him soon arose the powerful men who were traitors, first of all, Baldwin de Redvers and held Exeter against him; and the king besieged it, and afterwards Baldwin made peace. Then the others took and held their castles against him, and David, King of Scotland took to warring with him. Then, notwithstanding that, their messengers went between them, and they [Stephen and David] came together and were reconciled though it availed little.

1137.   In this year, King Stephen went over the sea to Normandy and there was received, because they thought that he should be just as his uncle was and because he still had his treasure; but he distributed and scattered it foolishly. King Henry had gathered much gold and silver, and no good did it me for his soul thereof.

When King Stephen returned to England, he then held his court at Oxford, and there he seized Roger, Bishop of Salisbury, and Alexander, Bishop of Lincoln; Roger, the Chancellor; his nephews and put all in prison until they gave up their castles. When the traitors perceived that he was a mild man and peaceable and good and did no justice, then they all did wonder. They had paid him homage, swore oaths, but they did not keep their promises; they all

committed perjury and did not keep their promises for
every powerful man made and held his castle against him
and filled the land full of castles. They greatly tormented
the wretched men of the land with castle building. When
the castles were made, then they filled [them] with devils
and evil men. Then they seized the men whom they thought
had any goods both by day and by night, men and women,
and put them in prison for [their] gold and silver, and
tormented them with unspeakable pains. For never were
any martyrs tormented as they were: they hung [them] up
by the feet and smoked them full of smoke; they hung
[them] by the thumbs, others by the head and hung coats
of armor on their feet. They had knotted ropes put about
their heads and twisted it until it went to the brain. They
put them in quarters in which were adders, snakes and
frogs and killed them so. Some they put into a torture
house, that is, into a chest which was short, narrow and
shallow and put sharp stones therein, and forced the men
therein so that they broke all their limbs. In many of the
castles, were snares and instruments of torture that were
chains that two or three men had enough to bear one, that
was so made that [they] were fastened to a beam and put
a sharp iron about the throat of the man and his neck so
that he might in no manner, sit or lie or sleep but bear all
that iron. Many thousands they killed by hunger.

I cannot nor may I tell all the wonders, nor all the pains
that they did to the wretched people of this land, and that
lasted nineteen winters while Stephen was king, and ever it
was worse and worse. They laid tribute on the towns, every
now and then and called it a special impost. When these
wretched men had no more to give, then they robbed and
burnt all their towns so that you might well go a whole
day's journey, you should never find a man sitting in a
town nor land tilled. Then was corn dear and meat and

cheese and butter, for no one was on the land. The wretched men died from hunger; some went on alms who were formerly rich men; some fled out of the land. [There] was never yet more wretchedness in the land and heathen men never did worse than they did; because everywhere afterward they spared neither church nor churchyard but seized all the goods that were therein and afterwards burnt the church and all together. They spared not the lands of the bishops, nor abbots, nor priests, but robbed monks and clerks and every other man whom [they] might anywhere. If two or three men came riding into town, all the township [would] flee from them, thinking that they were robbers. The bishops and the learned men ever cursed them but [it] was nothing to them thereof, because they were all accursed and forsworn and lost. Wheresoever they tilled, the earth bore no corn, because the land was all destroyed with such deeds, and they said openly that Christ slept and his saints. Such and more than we can say, we suffered nineteen winters for our sins.

In all this evil time, Martin, the abbot, held his abbacy for twenty winters, one half year and eight days with much trouble but provided for the monks and guests all that was fitting for them and held much charity in the house, and notwithstanding, worked on the church and set lands and rents thereto and greatly improved it and permitted [them] to roof it and brought them into the new monastery on St. Peter's massday with much solemnity. That was in the year of the Incarnation of Our Lord 1140, from the fire of the place 23. And he went to Rome, and there was well received by Pope Eugenius and there begot privileges, one of all the lands of the abbey and another of the lands which lie to the office of the churchwarden; and if he might live longer, he also intended to act from the office of treasurer. And he begot lands which powerful men had with strength;

from William Muldon who held the castle of Rockingham, he won Cottingham and Easton; and from Hugo of Waltville, he won Irthling and Stanwick; and sixty shillings each year from Aldwinkle. And he made many monks and planted vineyards and made many works and turned the town [into a] better [place] than it ever was, and was a good monk and a good man because he loved God and good men.

Now we shall say something of what happened in the time of King Stephen. In his time, the Jews of Norwich bought a Christian child before Easter and tortured him with all the same pains that Our Lord suffered, and on Good Friday [they] hanged him on a cross for the love of Our Lord and afterward buried him. [They] thought that it would be concealed but Our Lord showed that he was a holy martyr; and the monks took him and buried him with honor in the monastery, and he performed through Our Lord wonderful and manifold miracles, and he was called St. William.

1138.   In this year, David, King of Scotland, came with a very large army to this land, and against him came William, Earl of Albemarle, to whom the king had assigned York, and the other loyal men with a few men, and [they] fought them [the Scots] and put the king to flight at the Standards and killed very many of his gang.

1140.   In this year, King Stephen desired to take Robert, Earl of Gloucester, the son of King Henry, but he might not, because he [Robert] became aware of it. Thereafter, in the spring, the sun became dark and that day about noontime of the day became so dark that they lit candles to eat by and that was 13 days before the Kalends of April. Men became very frightened. Thereafter, William, Archbishop of Canterbury, died and the King made Theodore archbishop, who was an abbot in Bec [Normandy].

Thereafter very many wars followed between the King and Randolph, Earl of Chester, not because he did not give him all that he could ask for, as he did to all others, but ever the more he gave him, the worse he was to him. The Earl held Lincoln against the King and he took all that [he thought] he ought to have; and the King went thither and besieged him and his brother, William of Romare, in their castles. And the Earl stole out and went after Robert, Earl of Gloucester, and brought him thither with a great army and fought furiously on Candlemass day against their lord [King Stephen] and captured him—for his men deserted him and fled—and [they] led him to Bristol and there put him into prison and fetters. Then was all England stirred more than [it] ever was, and all evil was in the land.

Thereafter came the daughter of King Henry who had been Empress in Germany and was now Countess of Anjou and [she] came to London and the people of London desired to seize her and she fled and lost much there. Thereafter the Bishop of Winchester, Henry, the brother of King Stephen, spoke with Robert, the Earl, and the Empress, and swore oaths with them that he would never more hold with his brother, the King, and cursed all those men who held with him and told them that he would give up Winchester to them and made them come thither. When they were therein, then came the King's queen with all her strength and besieged them until there was much hunger within. So that they might not suffer long, they then stole out and fled; and they were aware without and followed them and took Robert, Earl of Gloucester, and led him to Rochester and put him into prison, and the Empress fled into a monastery. Then wise men went between friends of the King and friends of the Earl and made peace so that

they should let the King out of prison for the Earl and
the Earl for the King, and so [it] happened.

Afterwards the King and Randolph, Earl of Stanford,
made peace and swore oaths and made fast promises that
neither of them should betray the other. And it availed
nothing because the King took after him in Southampton
through wicked advice and put him into prison; and immediately he let him out through worse advice with the
agreement that he swear on the sacraments, and hostages
provided, that he should give up all his castles. Some he
gave up and some he did not give up, and did then worse
than he should here.

Then was England greatly divided. Some held with the
King, and some held with the Empress; for when the King
was in prison, the Earls and the powerful men thought that
he should never come out and made peace with the Empress and brought her into Oxford and gave her the
Borough. When the King was out, he heard this report and
took his army and besieged her in the tower; and they let
her down from the tower at night with ropes, and she stole
out and fled and went on foot to Wallingford. Thereafter
she went over the sea, and they of Normandy all went
from the King to the Earl of Anjou, some willingly and
some unwillingly, because he besieged them until they gave
up their castles and they never had help from the King.

Then Eustace, son of the King, went to France and took
the sister of the King of France to wife, thinking thereby to
get Normandy. But he profited little, and by good right
because he was an evil man, for the worse he became, the
more did he of evil than of good. He robbed the land and
laid on heavy taxes; he brought his wife to England and
put her in a castle in Canterbury; she was a good woman
but she had little happiness with him. And Christ willed

that he should not rule long, and he died, and his mother also.

And the Earl of Anjou died, and his son Henry took the kingdom. And the queen of France [Elenore] separated from the King [Louis VII] and came to the young Earl Henry, and he took her to wife and all Poitou with her. Then he went with a great army into England and won castles; and the King went against him with greater forces. And notwithstanding, they did not fight, because the Archbishop and the wise men went between them and made the agreement that the King should be lord and King while he lived, and after his day, Henry [should] become king; and he held him for a father and he him for a son and peace and accord should be between them and all England. This and the other agreements which they made, the King and the Earl and the Bishop and the Earls and all the powerful men swore to uphold. Then was the Earl received at Winchester and at London with much solemnity, and all did homage to him and swore to uphold the peace; and it soon became a very good peace as that never was before; and the Earl went over the sea and all the people loved him for he did good justice and made peace.

1154. In this year, King Stephen died and was buried where his wife and son were buried at Faversham [in Kent]; which monastery he made. When the King died, the Earl then was beyond the sea, and no one dared do anything but good because of great fear of him. When he came to England, then was he received with much dignity and consecrated King in London on the Sunday before midwinter's day and held a great court. That same day that Martin, the Abbot of the Borough, was to go thither, he then became sick and died on January 2, and the monks within the days chose another from themselves, William of

Walteville, was [he] called, a good cleric and a good man and well loved by the King and by all good men. And in the church, they buried the Abbot with great honor and soon the [newly] chosen Abbot went and the monks with him to Oxford to the King, and he gave him the office of the Abbot. And he took himself soon to Lincoln and was there consecrated Abbot before he came home; and afterward was received with much dignity at the Borough with many processions. And so he was also at Ramsay and at Thorney and Spalding and at S. I. born, and . . . , and [now is] Abbot and has begun fair. [May] Christ [give] him a good ending.

THE DEDICATION TO THE ORMULUM

Now, brother Walter, my brother after the flesh's kind,
And my brother in Christendom through baptism and
    through the vow,
And my brother in God's house yet [in] the third way,
Since we both have taken the rule to follow
Under the condition of canon and life just as St. Austin
    set;
I have done just as you bade and furthered thine will,
I have turned into English the lessons of the holy Gospels,
After the little wit that the Lord has lent to me.
Thou thought that it might well turn to much profit,
If the English people, for the love of Christ, would earnestly
    learn it
And follow it and fulfill it with thought, with word, and
    with deed;
And because you desired that I should work this work for
    you,
And I have furthered it for you, but all through the help
    of Christ,
And we both ought to thank Christ that it is brought to
    an end.
I have collected in this book nearly all of the Gospels
That are in the Massbook in all the year at Mass;
And ever after the Gospels remain that which the Gospel
    signifies,
That one ought to speak to the people of their soul's need;
And yet there you will find therein more than enough in
    addition,

Of that which the holy people of Christ ought to believe
    well and follow.
I have set here in this book among the words of the Gospels,
All by myself, many words as to fill the rime;
But you shall find that my word wherever there it is added,
May help those who read it to see and to understand
All this the better, how they ought to understand the
    Gospels.
And because I believe that you ought to bear my words
    well,
Everywhere where you shall find them among the words
    of the Gospels.
For whosoever might tell the lessons of the Gospel to the
    unlearned people,
He might well add many words among the words of the
    Gospel.
And I am not able, my verse always with Gospel words
To fill all well, and all therefore I shall often need
Among the words of the Gospel to put my words to fill
    out my verses.
    And I commit to you this book, the high duty as it seems,
Wholly to look through each one [of] the verses and to
    examine [them] often,
Because in this book is not one word against the teachings
    of Christ,
Not one word that may very well not be believed and
    followed.
We shall tread under foot and completely reject all
The judgments of all those evil people who are blinded by
    malice,
Who curse through sinful pride what is for praise.
They shall think contemptuously of our labor, dear brother,
And they all shall take it in vanity and frivolity,
But nothing by skill, but all by malice and by their sins.

And we ought to ask God that He forgive them their sins;
And we both ought to praise God from whom it was begun,
And to thank God that it was brought to an end through
   His help;
For it may help all those who hear it gladly,
And love it and follow it with thought, with word, with
   deed.
   And whosoever shall wish to write this book again an-
   other time,
I command him that he write it correctly, just as this book
   teaches him,
All completely after as it is in this first copy,
With all the same rimes as is here set down with all its
   many words;
And that he heeds well that he writes the letter of the
   alphabet twice
Everywhere where it is written in this book in that manner.
Heed he well that he writes it so, because he might nothing
   else
In English write the word correctly that he knows well in
   truth.
   And if any man wishes to know why I have done this
   deed,
Why I have turned the lessons of the holy Gospels into
   English,
I have done it because the salvation of all Christian people
Depends on that one [thing] that they, the lessons of the
   holy Gospels,
With full power, correctly follow in thought, in word, in
   deed.
For to follow ever all that on earth is the need of Christian
   people
I believe, in deed, all [this] teaches them the lessons of the
   holy Gospels;

And because whosoever learns it and follows it in deed,
He shall in the end be worthy through Christ to be saved.
And therefore I have turned it into the English speech,
Because I gladly desire that all the English people
Shall listen to it with [their] ears, shall believe it with
    [their] heart,
Shall speak it with [their] tongue, and shall follow it in
    deed,
To win under Christendom with God's truth their soul's
    salvation.
And if they will hear it and follow it in deed,
I have helped them under Christ to win their salvation.
And I shall have for my labor a good reward with God in
    the end,
If that I, for the love of God and for the reward of heaven,
Have turned for them into English for their soul's need.
And if they reject it all, it turns them to sin,
And I shall have gained for myself the favor of Christ the
    Lord,
Because of this, I have wrought this book for them for
    the need of their soul,
Because of this, they reject it all through their pride.
    The Gospels called in English by name is good word and
    good tidings,
God's message, because it was, through the Holy Gospel
    writers,
All wrought and written in the book of Christ's first coming,
Of how true God was become man for the need of mankind,
And from that, mankind was loosed out of Hell by His
    death,
And after that, He arose certainly the third day after death,
And after that, He certainly then ascended up to Heaven
    afterwards,

And after that, He shall come to judge all people,
And so to reward each man according to his own deeds.
Of all this good, the Gospel brings us the word and the
message and good tidings,
And so it may well be called the good message.
For man may find in the Gospel book the seven goodnesses
That Our Lord Jesus Christ has done for us on earth,
Because He came to man and because He became man on
earth.
  For the Lord Christ has done one goodness for us on
  earth,
Because He came to become man for the need of mankind.
The Lord Christ has done a second goodness for us on earth,
Because He was baptized in the river Jordan for our need;
Because He desired us [to be] kin by water through our
holy baptism,
Therefore He desired to be baptized Himself on earth in
water.
The Lord Christ has done the third goodness for us on earth,
Because He gave His own life with all His full will
To suffer death on the cross, innocent without blame,
To loosen mankind through His death out of the devil's
power.
The Lord Christ has done the fourth goodness for us on
earth,
Because His holy soul descended from the cross down to
Hell,
To take out of Hell all the good souls
Who had pleased Him in this life through true innocence.
The Lord Christ has done the fifth goodness for us on
earth,
Because He arose the third day from death for our good,
And allowed the Apostles to see Him in His human form;

Because He desired to strengthen also true faith in their
breast,
Therefore He, certainly in full truth, was risen from death,
And in the same flesh That was for us nailed to the cross;
Because He desired to strengthen well this truth in their
breast,
He allowed the Apostles to see Him well, and very often
afterwards on earth,
Within forty days after He arose from the dead.
The Lord Christ has done the sixth goodness for us on
earth,
Because He ascended for our good up into the bliss of
Heaven,
And sent afterwards the Holy Ghost to His disciples,
To comfort and encourage them to stand against the devil,
To give them good knowledge enough of all His holy
teachings,
To give them good desires, good strength to suffer all woe
All for the love of God, and not in order to win earthly
praise.
The Lord Christ shall yet do the seventh goodness for us in
the end,
Because He shall give us on Judgment Day the bliss of
Heaven,
If we shall be worthy to find God's grace.
    Thus Our Lord Christ has done seven goodnesses for us,
Because He came to man to become man on earth.
And in that holy book that is called the Apocalypse,
St. John, the Apostle, wrote for us through the teaching
of the Holy Ghost,
That he saw up in the heaven a book beset with seven seals,
And fastened so very well that it might not be open by
any person
Without God's Holy Lamb that he also saw in Heaven.

And through the seven seals was right very well betokened
That sevenfold goodness that Christ did for us through His
    coming;
And that no one might open the seven seals
Without God's Lamb that came in order that it shall
    betoken
That no one, no angel, no man, nor any kind of created
    thing,
Might through himself show those seven goodnesses
To mankind so that it might loosen mankind from Hell,
Nor give mankind pleasure, nor strength, to win the bliss
    of Heaven.
And all also the Lamb of God, all through His own
    strength,
Might easily and well enough open the seven seals,
Also the Lord Jesus Christ, all through His own strength,
With the Father and the Holy Ghost, one God and all one
    kind,
Also He right easily enough and well with all might
To mankind [might] show the seven seals through Himself,
So that He well enough might loosen mankind from Hell,
And give mankind life and pleasure and strength and wit
    and will,
To stand in to please God, to win the bliss of Heaven.
And therefore the holy Gospel book shows us all this
    goodness,
This sevenfold goodness that Christ did for us through His
    grace,
Because all Christian people are to follow the teachings of
    the Gospels.
And therefore have I turned it into English speech,
Because I desire gladly that all English people
With [their] ears shall listen to it, with [their] heart shall
    believe it,

With [their] tongue shall speak it, with deeds shall follow it,
To win under Christendom their soul's true salvation from
    Christ.
And Almighty God give us strength and pleasure and wit
    and will,
To follow this English book that is all holy teaching,
So that we might be worthy to enjoy the bliss of Heaven.
    Amen   Amen   Amen
  I who have set this in English, to teach Englishmen,
I was there, where I was christened, named Ormin by
    name;
And I, Ormin, full earnestly, with mouth and also with
    heart
Here bid the Christian men that hear or read
This book, I bid them here that they say this prayer for me,
That the brother who wrote and wrought first of all this
    English writing,
That the brother might find for his labors the reward of
    true bliss.

Amen

THE BESTIARY

The Lion's Nature

The lion stands on a hill; and he hears to hunt man,
Or through the smell of his nose smells that he draws near,
By which way he will turn downward so to the dale,
All his footsteps after him he fills;
Drags dust with his tail where he steps down,
Either dust or dew so that he [the hunter] cannot find him;
Drives down to his den where he will protect himself.
    Another trait he has. When he is born
Still lies the lion; not stirs he from sleep,
Until the sun has showed about him thrice;
Then his father raises him with the uproar that he makes.
    The third custom has the lion when he lies asleep
Never shall he close the lids of his eyes.

Signification

    Well high is that hill which is Heaven;
Our Lord is the lion who lives there above;
How then it pleased Him to alight here on earth,
Might never the devil know, because He is a secret hunter,
How He came down, nor how He sheltered Himself
In that gentle maiden, Mary by name,
Who bore Him to the profit of man.
    When Our Lord was dead, and buried also was His will,
In a grave He lay still until the third day;
His Father helped Him so that He arose from the dead
    then to hold us to life.
His will so watches us, as a shepherd for his flock;

He is [the] shepherd, we are [the] sheep; He will protect us
If we hear also His word so that we go nowhere wrongly.

The Eagle's Nature

I will make known the eagle's nature
As I read it in a book;
How he restores his youth,
How he comes out of [old] age,
After his limbs become unwieldly,
After his beak is all awry,
After his flight is all weak,
And his eyes dim.
Hear how he renews himself;
A well he seeks that flows ever,
Both by night and by day;
Thereover he flies and up he goes
Until that he sees the heavens,
Through skies six and seven,
Until he comes to heaven.
So right as he knows
He tarries in the sun;
The sun burns all his flight,
And except it makes his eyes bright,
His feathers fall from the heat,
And he down with [the feathers] to the water
Falls into the bottom of that well.
There he becomes hale and hearty,
And comes out all new,
Were not his beak untrue.
His beak is yet wrong as before,
Though his limbs are strong,
He may not obtain food for himself
Nor any good for himself.
Then he goes to a stone,

And he pecks with his bill thereon,
Pecks with his bill until his beak [as] before
Has the distortion lost;
Afterward with his right bill
He takes the meat that he desires.

Signification

Every man is as is the eagle, will you now listen,
Old in his secret sins before he becomes a Christian.
And thus he renews himself, this man, when he is taken to
    church;
Before he can think of it, his eyes were dark;
[He] forsakes there Satan and every sinful deed,
Takes himself to Jesus Christ for He shall be his reward,
Believes in Our Lord Christ and learns the priests' lore;
From his eyes the mist goes away, while he tarries there.
His hope is all towards God and of His love he thinks,
That is the sun certainly, thus his sight he remedies,
Falls naked into the baptismal font and comes out all new,
Except a little; what is that? His mouth is yet untrue,
His mouth is yet very much unacquainted with the pater-
    noster and the credo.
Fare he north or fare he south, he shall learn his need;
Saying prayer to God and thus his mouth becomes right,
To aid him as food for the soul through the grace of Our
    Lord.

The Serpent's Nature

A serpent is in the world, well man knows it,
Adder is the name; thus he renews himself
When he is worn out, and in his old age all corrupt.
[He] fasts ten full days until his skin loosens itself,
So that he is thin and powerless and hardly might move;
He creeps forth crippled, his power thus he shows,

Seeks a stone that a hole is in, [it is] narrow but he forces
    himself,
Going with difficulty for his skin he leaves there.
His flesh creeps forth, walks towards the water,
To drink then awhile. But he spews out before all the poison
That was bred in his breast from his birthtime;
[He] drinks enough after and thus he renews himself.
    When the adder is in his naked skin
And bare of his breast poison,
If he naked sees a man, he will not draw near him,
But he flees from him as he should from a fire.
If he clothed sees a man, he becomes bold,
For he straightens himself up, ready to destroy,
To destroy or to make dead, if he might effect it.
What if the man becomes aware and were able to drive
    him away,
Fights with this serpent and goes on fighting him?
This adder afterwards he shall, of necessity,
Make a shield with his body and shield his head;
Little [concerned] for his limbs is he, but he keeps his life.

Signification

    Know, Christian man, what you promised Christ
At the churchdoor where you were christened.
You promised to believe in Him and to love His laws,
To keep in your heart the commandments of Holy Church.
If you have broken them, you pervert all,
Perish, and eternal life to possess fades away;
Enfeebled art [thou] in eternal bliss as the serpent is in the
    world.
Renew thyself as the adder does,
It is thy need.
Strengthen thyself with steadfastness and [be] full of virtues,
And help the poor men who go about.

Judge thyself not of any worth that you dare to look
Up towards Heaven; but walk on the earth
Mildly among men. You [should] know no pride,
Pride nor the vice of men; but desist from sinning,
And for salvation, ask you ever for yourself, both by night
    and by day,
So that you might have mercy for your misdeeds.
This life betokens the path that the adder goes by,
And this is the hole in the stone that you shall go through:
Loosen thy filth from thee as the serpent does his skin;
Go thou then to God's house to hear the Gospel
That is drink for the soul, quenching sins.
But before thou tell thy sins in confession to the priest,
Cleanse thyself thus of thy breast poison and strengthen
    thyself always,
Firmly in thy heart what you promised firmest.
Thus art thou young and renewed, always be thou true.
You need not [fear] the devil, for he may not destroy any-
    thing of thee;
But he flees from thee as the naked serpent from thee.
In the clothing, the adder is bold, and the devil adheres in
    sins;
Ever the sinful will he beset,
And with mankind he has contention and gain.
What if he has permission from the Heavenly Lord
In order to destroy us as he did our elders before?
We use the body in the struggle and protect the soul,
That is like our head, keep we it worthily.

The Whale's Nature

The whale is a fish
The largest that is in the water;
That you will see yet,
If you saw it when it floats,

That it were an island
That sets on the sea sand.
   This fish that is rough,
When he is hungry, he gapes wide;
Out of his throat there goes an odor
The sweetest thing that is in the land.
Therefore other fishes follow him,
When they smell it, they are glad;
They come and hover in his mouth,
Of his craftiness, they are ignorant.
Then this fish closes his jaws,
Sucking in all these fishes;
The small ones he will thus deceive,
The great ones he might not catch.
   This fish lives at the bottom of the sea,
And lives there ever hale and hearty,
Until it comes the time
That a storm stirs up all the sea,
When summer and winter strive.
He may not live therein,
So disturbed is the bottom of the sea,
He may not live there at that time,
But stirs up and tarries still.
While the weather is so bad,
The ships that are tossed on the sea,—
Unwelcome to them is death and pleasant to live,—
Look about them and see the fish,
An island they think it is.
Thereof they are very [much] pleased,
And with their might they draw thereto
To fasten on the ship,
And all go up [on this fish.]
From the stone against steel in the tinder
Well to burn on this wonder,

They warm themselves well and eat and drink.
The fire he feels and does sink with them,
For soon he dives down to the bottom;
He kills them all without a wound.

Signification

The devil is powerful with will and might
As witches have in their craft;
He makes men to be hungry and to have a thirst,
And many other sinful lusts,
He attracts men to him with his deceptions,
Whosoever follows him, he finds ignominy.
Though the little ones are in pleasant customs,
The great ones he might not draw to himself;
The great, I mean, the steadfast
In right belief in flesh and spirit.
Whosoever listens to the teachings of the devil,
At length, it shall make him sorely sorry;
Whosoever fastens hope on him,
He shall follow him to dim Hell.

THE STORY OF JOSEPH

Potiphar believed his wife's tale,
And had judged Joseph guilty;
He commanded [him] to be fastened down fast,
And held cruelly in prison.
In the little time while he was there,
The keeper of the prison so began to love him,
And had him assigned in the prison,
To live in care of the prisoners.
    Either for a misdeed or for an accusation,
There was dragged to that prison
One who had charge of the king's cup,
And another who made the king's bread.
Both of them dreamed a dream in the night,
And they became very much afraid.
Joseph served them there regularly
At their drink and at their meal;
He heard them mourning, he asked them wherefore;
Cruel dreams possess that power.
Then he said to the butler,
    "Tell me your dream, my brother dear;
Whether so it becomes mild or strong,
The good interpretation belongs to God."
    "I dreamed that I stood at a vine,
That had grown three boughs;
At first it bloomed and afterward bore,
I became aware, the ripe berries.
The king's cup I had in my hand;
The berries therein I thought I pressed,
And brought it to the Pharaoh to drink,

I dreamt as I was wont to do."

"It is good," said Joseph, "to dream of wine,
Happiness and joy are therein;
Three days are yet to come,
You shall be taken out of prison,
And set again in your office.
Think you of me when it shall be;
Bring my message to the Pharaoh,
So that I might be taken out of prison;
For I was stolen from [my] native land
And unjustly held in bondage."

Said the baker, "Listen now to me:
I dreamed I bore three bread baskets
And therein bread and other food
Which the king is wont to eat;
And the birds have seized thereon,
Therefore I am in sorrow and care,
For I might not defend myself at all
Nor that food take from them."

"It is more pleasant," said Joseph,
"Of happy dreams to interpret the meaning;
You shall after the third day,
Be going on a journey, alas!
And birds shall tear your flesh to pieces
So that no power shall be able to defend you."

The truth happened as Joseph said it.
The butler soon forgot Joseph;
Two years afterward Joseph was fasten
There in prison without a home.
Then King Pharaoh dreamed a dream
That he stood by a river in flood,
And thence out came seven cows,
Each one, indeed, very fat and large;
And seven lean ones after them,

Which put the seven fat ones in woe.
The lean ones have eaten the fat ones;
This dream the king may not forget.
And other dreams came before him:
Seven ears of corn grew fat,
On a strong stalk and well grown,
And seven lean ones right thereby,
Withered and small and the drought took,
The strong have overcome them;
Together they went and in a moment
The fat ones dropped to the ground.
The king sprang up and awoke in thought,
Of the meaning of these dreams he knew nothing;
Nor was there one so wise in all the land
Who knew to undo the bonds of these dreams.
   Then that butler thought of himself
Of what he dreamed there in prison,
And of Joseph in the prison,
And he told it to Pharaoh the king.
Joseph was soon sought then in prison,
And shaved and clothed and brought to him.
The king asked him to be hardy and bold,
If he could tell the meaning of these dreams;
He told him what he dreamed at night,
And Joseph expounded his dreams very well.
   "These two dreams are both one,
God wishes to show thee, King Pharaoh.
Since the seven years are yet to come,
In all abundance shall they be taken,
And seven others shall be after,
Sorry and needful, men shall see them,
All that these first seven [years] make
Shall the other seven destroy and take away.
I advise, thee, King, now in respect to this,

To make barns and gather corn,
That thy people will not be taken unawares
When the years of hunger are forthcoming."
    King Pharaoh listened to his advice,
That became for him afterwards good fortune.
He delivered his ring to Joseph,
And his bracelet of gold for honor,
And requested him to look after all his land
And for to be [the] highest [one] under him;
And asked him to manage in his hand
His people, his affairs, and all his land.
    Then was under him this Potiphar,
And his wife who caused him so [much] trouble.
Joseph took his daughter to wife,—
Another [condition] is now than had happened before;—
And she bore him there two children,
Before men became aware of that hunger,
First Manasseh and Ephraim;
They loved God, He repaid them for it.
The seven fulsome years went,
Joseph knew to take precaution in respect to this;
When corn was wanting in other lands,
Then was enough under his hands.
    Hunger grew in the land of Canaan
And Jacob thereupon his ten sons
Sent into Egypt to get corn;
He left at home who was the youngest born.
The ten came, driven by necessity,
To Joseph and they knew him not.
And then they bowed to him timidly,
And said to him humbly,
    "We are messengers, driven by need,
To buy corn thereby to live."
    Joseph knew them all in his thought,

Yet he pretended he knew them not.
　"It seems indeed that you are spies
And came into this land to spy;
And came you for no other thing
But to spy on our lord the King."
　"No," they said, each one,
"Spies were we never any,
But we are all sons of one father;
Because of hunger do we come hither."
　"But now I know you are spies,
For by your bearing, men may see it.
How should one poor man forget
So and so many sons beget?
For seldom [does it] happen to any King himself
Such men to see of his offspring."
　"Ah, lord, mercy, there is yet another,
He might not go from his father.
He is the youngest, called Benjamin,
For we are all of the Hebrew race."
　"Now, by the faith I owe to King Pharaoh,
You all shall not hither go,
Until you bring me Benjamin,
The youngest brother of your family."
　For then was Joseph sorely frightened
That he was wronged but through them.
He did bind them and led [them] down
And fastened [them] firmly in prison;
The third day he let them go,
All but that one brother, Simeon;
This Simeon remained there in bond
To be a pledge in Joseph's hand.
　These other brothers soon anon
Took leave and went home.
And soon they were gone thither,

They very sorely have lamented him
And said among themselves,
    "Deservedly we are in sorrow,
For we sinned once before
Against our brother much more,
For we refused him mercy,
Now, therefore, we endure all sorrow."
It turned not about them in his mind,
But Joseph understood it all.
    Joseph's men then did at once
All as Joseph had commanded them;
Then he had the brothers' sacks filled,
And in each one put the silver
That they had paid for the corn
And bound the mouths [of the sacks] before them.
But the brothers knew it not,
How this deed was wrought;
But they all were amazed,
And had brought it thus to Jacob,
And told him thus of their fortune;
And he listened to all of it in fear.
When the men unbound these sacks there
And in the corn found the money,
They were then all sorely afraid.
Jacob thus bemoaned them aright,
    "Indeed, much sorrow has come to me,
Because my two children are taken away from me.
Of Joseph I know not the ending,
And bonds are laid on Simeon;
If you take Benjamin from me,
Death and sorrow [will] fall to me.
Ever shall Benjamin remain with me
There while I shall live in this world."

Then Judas said, "[It] shall be difficult for us
If we do not hold to our agreement with him."
   Scarcity grew, this corn is gone,
Jacob afterwards bids them to go again;
But they dared not go on the way,
   "Unless you send Benjamin with us."
Then said he, "When it is necessary,
And I know no better counsel,
Take all that silver again
That they wanted not thereof,
And other silver before them
In order to buy other corn with;
Fruits and spices of dear price
Take to that man who is so wise.
God grant him to be gracious,
And send me my children again."
Then they took [their] departure immediately,
Until they were alight in Egypt.
And when Joseph saw them all,
Kind thoughts lay in his heart.
He commanded his steward to prepare his food,
He said they should eat with him.
He led them all to Joseph's city,
None of them had then a merry countenance.
   "Lord," they said then each one,
"Your silver is returned to you again;
It was put into our sacks,
No guilt therein known to us."
   "Be quiet now," said the steward,
"For I now have my orders."
   Then came that brother Simeon
And kissed his brothers one by one;
Very glad was he of their coming,

For he was taken there as a hostage.
It was late morning or later,
Home came that rich lord there;
And all those brothers in a fearful mind,
Fell before that lord's foot,
And gave him rich presents,
That their father had sent to him.
And he gladly understood it,
For they were all of the same blood.
    "Lives," said he, "that father yet
Who thus begot so many sons?"
    "Lord," they said, "yet he lives—"
Know I then none that they did not tremble,—
"And this is young Benjamin
Brought thither according to thy message."
    When Joseph saw them before him,
By father and mother born brothers,
His heart turned over in him immediately;
Natural love began to overcome him.
Soon he went out and quietly wept,
So that all his face became wet with tears.
After that weeping he washed his face.
And he then came in and asked them to eat.
He did wash them and before him
Sat them down as they were born;
Yet he thought of his father's house,
How he sat at the meal with his sons.
Of every course of dinner, of every wine,
He gave Benjamin the most and the best.
In the plenty, he became glad,
Joseph thought therefore of no harm,
But it pleased him very well.
And [he] instructed and taught [them] well

And how they should act best
When they came into a strange country;
"And all the better shall you fare,
If you conduct yourselves with truth."
Afterwards in the morning when it was day,
Before the brothers went away,
Their sacks were all filled with corn,
And the silver [put] in [as] before;
And the sack that Benjamin had
Therein was hidden Joseph's cup.
And when they were gone out of town,
Joseph had them sent after.
These messengers overtook them quickly,
And accused [them] of wrong and evil;
"Unhappy men, what have you done?
Great misfortune has come to you,
For it is not concealed from my lord
That one of you has stolen his cup."
Then the brothers said truly,
"Upon whom you find it surely,
He [will] be killed and we driven back
To live evermore in slavery."
They began to ransack them one by one,
And found it there soon anon;
And took every one of the brothers
And led them back sorrowfully,
And brought them before Joseph
With sad countenance, sorrow and weeping.
Then Joseph said, "Do you not know
That I am very wise in thought?
Nothing may be concealed from me very long
Whatsoever is stolen in this land."
"Lord," said Judas, "Do with me

Whatsoever thy will be in this world,
Provided that you free Benjamin.
I led him out on my pledge
That he would come back again
To his father and be with him."
  Then much sadness came upon Joseph,
He had all the others sent out;
And spoke with difficulty as he wept,
So that all his face became wet with tears.
  "I am Joseph, fear ye not,
For your safety or [why you were] brought hither.
Two years is [it] now that the scarcity has come.
Yet shall five full [years more] be taken,
That men shall not sow nor reap,
So shall the drought destroy the fields.
Hasten you to your father again,
And tell him what my blessings are;
And make him come hither to me,
And you and your property all together.
On good pastures in the land of Goshen
You shall have separate realms.
Everyone he kissed, over each he wept,
Each of them was wet with his tears.
  Soon it was made known to King Pharaoh,
How this new message did happen;
And he was happy, glad in heart,
That Joseph would bring them hither,
For the love of Joseph, might he prosper.
He commanded [them] to take carts and wagons,
And to fetch their wives, children and men,
And gave them there all the land of Goshen,
And promised them that they should have
More and better [things] than they were able to desire.

Joseph gave each of them two garments,
Benjamin he made most proud;
Benjamin bore five of the best garments,
And three hundred pieces of fine silver.
Also many other things thereto
He asked to be in his father's will;
And ten asses with firm horse loads
Of all Egypt, the best wealth
Gave he his brothers with a glad heart
And asked them to hasten themselves homeward quickly;
And he did so with a glad heart;
Towards their father they began to go,
And when they came before him,
He knew not who they were.

"Lord," they said, "of Israel,
Joseph thy son greets thee well,
And sends the message that he lives;
All Egypt belongs in his will."

Jacob sprang up and believed it not
Until he saw all that brought wealth.

"Well for me," he said, "well, [it] is indeed,
That I have thus waited for such a time.
And I shall go to my son,
And see [him] before I go from the world."
Jacob went out of the land of Canaan
And of his race very many a man.
Joseph understood them very well
And Pharaoh thought it very good.
Because they were shepherds,
He asked them to be in the land of Goshen.

Jacob was brought before the King
In order to give his blessing.

"Father dear," said Pharaoh,

"How many years are in thee?"
"One hundred years and thirty more
Have I here in the world endured woe;
Though I think few thereof
When I have endured them in woe,
After I began to be in the world,
Here without home, mankind between."
So thinks every wise man
Who knows how mankind began,
And who remembers the guilt of Adam,
That he lives here without a dwelling.
    Pharaoh bade him to be well
In soft rest and good time;
He and his sons remained at rest
In the land of Goshen in different places.
Afterwards there was made a city
Which was called Rameses;
Jacob alive lived there
At rest full fourteen years;
And God let him see beforehand
Which time his ending should be.
He asked of Joseph, his dear son,
One thing that he remember well of [him,]
That when it would be done with him,
He should bury him in Hebron;
And surely he had it said to him
The place where Abraham was laid.
So he was pleased to be laid
Where the Holy Ghost had quietly told
Him and his elders long ago before,
Where Jesus Christ would be born
And where be killed and where be buried;
He thought to have rest with them.

Joseph swore to him all that he asked,
And he became happy and glad thereof.
Before he was then to go from the world,
He asked his people to come to him,
And told [them] what should be for them;
The Holy Ghost made it seen to him.
In a clean ending and a holy life,
So left he this world's strife.

Joseph did prepare his fair body,
Washed [it] and anointed [it] richly,
And perfumed [it] sweetly with spices;
And the Egyptian people watched over him
Forty nights and forty days;
Such were the Egyptian customs.
The first nine nights [were] to wash the body,
And to anoint and to wind and to lament.
And to watch over it was for forty nights;
The men did so who had strength.
And the Hebrew people had a custom,
Not soon to bury it with iron,
But to wash it and keep it right
Without ointment for seven nights,
And afterwards anoint it for thirty days.
Christian people have other customs;
They are anointed therefore while they live,
With chrism and oil, given in faith;
For with faith and good deeds
Is done then all that watching.
Some one, some three, some seven nights
Some thirty, some twelve months exactly,
And some every [so often] prepare for years,
The while that they live here;
They do for their death, churchgoing,

Almsgiving, and songs of the Mass,
And that is in place of the watch;
Well may [it] be with him who did it well.
The Egyptian people have him waked
For forty nights and make feasts,
And his sons thirty days,
In a clean life and holy customs.
   So were gone passed ten weeks,
Yet Jacob had burial none.
And the message came to King Pharaoh,
What Joseph had sworn to his father.
And he granted to him for he did well,
And commanded him to take him with companions,
Well armed and wise in war,
So that no man harm them along the way.
That bier is led, the people are told,
They go about by Atad.
Full seven nights they remain there,
And bemoan for Jacob dead.
So long have they thence taken,
To the river Jordan that they are come,
And over Paran to Hebron;
There is the body placed in burial.
And Joseph went into Egypt
With all his people sent out with him.

FLORIS AND BLANCHEFLEUR

The porter thought what to advise;
He remembered to gather flowers in the meadow,
He remembered to fill baskets of flowers
To scatter in the maidens' bower.
That was his advice to help him so,
He permitted Floris to go into that one basket.
Two maids bore the basket,
And because [it was] heavy, they were angry;
They asked God to give him an evil end
Who put so many flowers therein.
To the chamber where they should go
They did not go aright;
To another chamber they have gone,
Not to Blanchefleur's chamber.
They set the basket on the ground,
And went away and left it for a time.
    One maiden came and wished
To see and handle the flowers;
Floris thought it was his sweet one,
Out of the basket he leaped aright,
And that maid for fear
Began to cry and scream.
Then Floris knew not what to say
For the terror that he had;
Into the basket he started again
And in the flowers he hid.
This maid thought right away
That it was Floris, that sweet one,
For her chamber was near,

Seldom were they that near together,
And often had Blanchefleur told her
How she was sold from him.

Now maidens came leaping to her
Well fifteen in one heap,
And asked her what was with her,
And why she made such a noise.
Indeed she was discreet and [considered] where
To find an answer for them:

"To the basket," she said, "I came and wished
To see and handle the flowers;
There flew out a butterfly,
Before I knew [it] into my eye,
So sorely was I afraid of it
That I began to cry aloud."
These others laughed and had glee
And went back and let [her] be.

Clarice is named that gracious maid;
To Blanchefleur she began to go,
And said, "Sweet Blanchefleur,
Will you see a very fair flower?
It grew not in this land,
The flower that I bring thee in hand."

"Away, Clarice," said Blanchefleur,
"Who that loves as a lover,
And has joy thereof, may love flowers;
But I live in sorrow in this tower,
For I think without jest,
That the amir will have me.
But that day shall never be,
Nor shall men ever blame me
That I am untrue in love,
Nor change love for a new one,

Nor leave the old be, for a new one,
So does Floris in his country;
   "Although this Floris forget me
I shall never forget him."
Clarice heard this bad sorrow
Of trust and of faith;
The tears ran down her cheeks;
   "Blanchefleur," she said, "good companion,
Dear sweet Blanchefleur,
Come and see a very fair flower."

   Together now they go certainly,
And Floris has heard all this;
Out of the basket he leaps anon,
And to Blanchefleur he began to go.
Each soon knew the other,
They both now change [their] hue;
Together without word they sprang,
Embraced and kissed and also wept;
Their kissing lasted a long time,
And that seemed to them a little while.

   When Clarice beheld all this,
Their countenances and their joy;
Said Clarice to Blanchefleur,
   "Know you anything in this flower?
A little before you did not wish to see it,
Now it might not be loosened from thee.
He must know much of art
That you would give thereof a part."

   "Certainly," said Blanchefleur to Clarice,
This is my own sweet Floris."

   Now both of these two sweet things
Cried for her mercy all weeping,
That she might not betray them to the amir,

For then was their sorrow near.
Clarice had pity on them.
    "Nothing," she said, "fear ye,
Fear ye not anymore withal
That it should happen through me.
I shall conceal and betray nothing
Of the company of you two."
    Clarice had brought them to bed
That was wrought with costly cloth and silk;
Into the bed she laid them down,
And took herself from them.
Then Floris first began to speak;
    "Our Lord," he said, "who made man
I thank thee, the Son of God,
That I have come to my love.
My love, now have I found thee,
Of all my cares I am unburdened."
    Now each has told the other
Of their sorrows and cold cares,
That they both had found
Since they were separated in two.
Now they embraced and kissed,
And made together much joy;
If there was anything without virtue
Sweet Blanchefleur knew it.
No other heaven did they pray for
Except ever to lead such a life.
    But not for long might they keep themselves
So that they [might] not be perceived,
For the amir had such a habit,
Each morning there must come
Two maidens with much honor
Up to the highest tower,

Who were fair and very gracious;
The one in order to comb his head,
The other to bring towel and basin
In order to wash his hands in.
Such served him one day so fair,
Tomorrow must come another pair.
But mostly were called into the tower
Maid Clarice and Blanchefleur.

Clarice, her joy must happen,
Rose up in the early morning,
And has called Blanchefleur
To go with her into the tower.
Said Blanchefleur, "I am coming,"
But she said it all sleeping.
Clarice came into the tower;
The amir asked for Blanchefleur.

"Sir, all night at her book
She has looked and read,
And therein prayed her prayer
That God who suffered the passion
Hold thee, Sir, in long life;
And now she is fast asleep
So that she might not come to thee."

"Is that the truth?" said he.
She said, "Yes, Sir, without lying."

"She is," he said, "a sweet thing,
Indeed, have I wished her to wife,
Who prays for my life so earnestly."

In the morning Clarice arose
She blamed Blanchefleur
That she made so long delay.

"Arise," she said, "and we [will] go together."
Said Blanchefleur, "I come anon."

But Floris began to embrace her,
And she also him unwisely,
And fell asleep in this way.

When Clarice came to the pillar,
And took the basin of gold
To bear with her into the tower,
She looked for Blanchefleur.

When Clarice came into the tower,
He asked for Blanchefleur.

"Sir, I thought to find her here,
She was arisen as I was;
Has she not come yet?"
He said, "She fears me too little."

He called his chamberlain to him,
And commanded him to go with all might
In order to learn why she came not
At his behest very soon.

Forth he went soon anon,
So that he came to her chamber.
In her bed, he found two,
Indeed, firmly embraced, both asleep
Face to face and mouth to mouth;
Soon were their sorrows known.

To the amir soon he went
And told him what he saw.
The amir commanded him to bring his sword;
Learn of this thing he would.
Forth he went with all his might,
He and his chamberlain;
In the bed he found two,
The sleep was still in their eyes.
He did cast down the bed clothes
Below the breast;

By their breast, he knew anon
That one was a maid and the other a man.
   The children awoke then immediately
And saw the amir going before them
With his sword drawn out;
Sorely afraid were they and indeed [they] might be.
   "Say," said the amir, "fair friend,
Who made thee so bold
As to come into my tower
And to lie with Blanchefleur?"
They cried to him for mercy, both quickly,
That he give them time to live.
   After his baronage, he has sent
To avenge him with their judgment,
And did bind them fast at the time
And into prison be cast.
His palace that was so fairly built
Of Earls and Barons was it filled.
Up he stood among them all,
In appearance very angry withal;
   "Lords," he said, "With much honor
You have heard of Blanchefleur
How I bought her on my faith
For seven times her weight in gold;
In her was my greatest hope
In order to have for my queen.
It was not long after that I came in,
And found her in adultery,
To shame and dishonor me
In her bed in my tower.
I have told you how it has happened;
Avenge me with a judgment."
   Then spoke a free citizen

Who was gracious and courteous;
   "Sir, before they are sentenced to death,
We might hear the children speak;
There is nothing else right in judgment
Without answer to the accusation."
   The King of Nubia then said,
"In truth, it shall not go thus;
It is right through all things
For felons taken red-handed
For to suffer judgment
Without answer to the other's accusation."
   The men now sent for the children;
The men kindled a fire to burn them.
Said Floris to Blanchefleur,
"For our life there is no succour,
But mine is the guilt and the error
That you shall suffer death for me;
But if nature might suffer it,
I ought to die twice by right,
One death for thee, another for me.
For you suffer this now for me.
For if I had not come into this tower,
With mirth, you might live herein."
   He drew forth a rich ring
His mother gave him at his parting:
   "Have the ring, my dear one,
You might not die while it is thine."
The ring he has reached forth
And delivered to Blanchefleur.
   "The ring shall never save me,
For death may I never see in thee."
The ring she desires to hand back
And deliver it to Floris;

But for all that she might do,
He would not take it back again,
And the ring at one time
Fell down upon the ground.
A duke stooped and picked it up,
And was thereof a very happy man.
  Now the men bring the children forth
To their doom all weeping,
But there was not so stern [a] man
Who looked at them,
Who would not be truly glad
That the judgment be withdrawn;
For Floris was so fair a youth,
And Blanchefleur so sweet a thing,
Of men and women that are now,
That go and see and speak with mouth,
Were not so fair in their gladness
As they were in their sorrow.
But the amir was so mad and angry
He shook from anger where he stood,
And commanded to bind them very firmly
And cast [them] into the fire.
  The duke who found the ring
Came to the amir and whispered,
And all together they began to show him
By whom the children were known.
The amir had them called back,
For he would speak with Floris.
  "Sir," said Floris, "in truth I say
You ought not kill the maid;
For all this guilt I am to blame,
I ought to die and she go free."
Said Blanchefleur, "Kill thou me,

And let Floris be alive;
If it were not for my love
He would not [have] come from his land."
The amir said, "So I must go,
You shall both die together;
I myself will avenge myself,
You shall never go nor speak."
   Floris offered forth his neck,
And Blanchefleur pulled him back again;
Blanchefleur offered forth her neck,
And Floris began to strive with her again.
Neither might suffer there
That the other die before.
Then the amir though he was angry,
He there changed his countenance;
For either would die for the other,
And he saw many weeping eyes,
And because he loved that maid so much,
All weeping he turned away.
His sword fell from his hand to the ground,
He might not hold it at that time.
   The duke that had their ring,
He had a wish to speak for them;
   "Sir, amir," said he, "certainly
It is of very little profit
For to kill these fair children;
But it is better that he tell you
How he came into thy tower
To lie there with Blanchefleur.
His skill when you know it
The better with others you might know it."
   All who heard his words
Beseeched that he grant this.

He commanded him to tell his method,
How he came in to Blanchefleur,
And who advised and helped thereto.
"That," said he, "I shall never do
For things that men may do to me,
Except it be forgiven them also."
All the others beseeched this,
And by the amir [it] is granted.
    Now the beginning and the end he has told them;
How Blanchefleur was sold from him,
How he was the son of the King of Spain
Come thither for the love of her.
To try with some method
How he might win her;
And how through the basket and the bribe,
The porter had become his man,
And how he was borne in the basket.
All the others therefore laughed.
    Then the amir, indeed it happened,
He sat those children by his side;
And has forgiven both of his wrath,
Floris and Blanchefleur too,
And said they should be to him
The best of all his retinue.
And Floris he made to stand upright
And there dubbed him to a knight.
Now both these children together for happiness
Fell to his feet to kiss them;
He allowed to bring them to a church,
And to wed them with a golden ring.
Upon the advice of Blanchefleur
Men fetched Clarice down from the tower.
The amir took her for his queen;

This festival was indeed excellent,
For there were all the happy relatives
Who might be at any bridal.
   It was not long thereafter
That there came writing and a message to Floris,
That his father the King was dead
And that he should follow its advice.
Then the amir said,
"If you act on my advice,
Remain with me and turn not home;
I will give you a kingdom
All as long and all as broad,
As ever yet your father commanded."
   But Floris would not for any pleasure [do this].
[It was] more pleasant for him [to be] with his kin.
   He bid good-bye to the amir,
And thanked Clarice, that fair maid,
And he has given to her
Twenty pounds of ready gold;
And to Daris who so taught him,
Twenty pounds he handed,
And all who did any thing for him
He paid them very well at the time.
He commended them all to God Almighty,
And came home when he might.
He was King with much honor,
And she his queen, Blanchefleur.
   Now you have heard the end
Of Floris and his gracious mistress,
How after calamity came good.
God grant that [it] might [be] so with us,
That we might love Him so
That we might to heaven go.   Amen.

THE DEBATE OF THE BODY AND THE SOUL

As I lay on a winter's night
   In a dejected mood before the day,
Indeed, I saw a holy sight,
   A body on a bier lay,
That had been a proud knight
   And little served God to satisfaction;
Lost he had the light of life,
   The soul was out and should away.

When the soul it should go,
   It turned around and stood by,
To behold the body where it came from
   So sorrowfully with dreadful mind;
It said, "Woe and alas!
   Who honors thy flesh, thy foul blood.
Wretched body why are you lying so,
   That once was so wild and mad?

"You who was wont to ride
   High on a horse in and out,
So skillful a knight known so wide,
   As a lion fierce and proud,
Where is all thy mighty pride,
   And thy speech which was so loud?
Why lie you there so bare on the side
   Clothed in that poor shroud?

"Where are thy costly clothes,
   Thy sumpter horses with thy rich trappings,

Thy proud palfreys and thy steeds
 That thou led around in thy right hand?
Thy falcons that were wont to cry out,
 And thy hounds that you fed?
I think God is too stingy to thee,
 So that all thy friends are fled from thee.

"Where are thy castles and thy towers,
 Thy chambers and thy rich halls
Painted with such rich flowers,
 And thy rich robes all?
Thine quilts and thy bedclothes,
 Thy rich cloth and thy rich apparels?
Wretch, now is thy bower very dark;
 Tomorrow thou shall fall therein.

"Where are thine active cooks,
 That should go to prepare thy food
With spices sweet for to smell,
 So that you were never full of food
To make that foul flesh to swell
 That foul worms shall eat?
And you have the pains of Hell
 Begot for me with gluttony . . ."

"For God created thee after His image,
 And gave thee both intelligence and reason;
In thy care was I left
 To be guided by thine will.
I never took up witchcraft,
 Nor knew I what was good or evil,
Except as a dumb and stupid wretch,
 Except as you taught me thereof.

"Set to serve thee for pleasure
  Both in the evening and in the morn,
Since I was assigned to guard thee,
  From the time that you were born.
You that could judge deeds
  Should have been aware before
Of my folly, as it seems;
  Now with this self thou are lost."

The soul it said, "Body, be still!
  Who has taught thee all this knowledge
Who gives me these harsh words,
  Who lies there swollen as a bottle?
Think thou, wretch, though thou fill
  A pit with thy foul flesh,
Of all the deeds thou did badly
  That thou so lightly shall be quiet?

"Think thou now to get the peace
  Where you lie rotting in the clay?
Though you be rotten outside and inside,
  And blown away by the wind,
Yet shall you come with limb and joint
  Again to me on Judgment Day,
And come to court, I with thee,
  In order to await our hard sentence.

"You were assigned to me to teach;
  But when you thought of the evil,
You laughed at the bridal in your teeth,
  You did all that I forbid you.
To sin and shame was it thy tendency,
  To evil and to wickedness;

Enough I stood against [thee] and fought,
But you always took your own advice.

"When I would instruct and teach thee
What was evil and what was good,
No speech was of Christ nor of the Church,
But [you] ran about and acted mad;
Enough I might preach and pray,
I might never turn thy mind
So that you would recognize God,
But [you] did all that your heart [was] inclined to.

"I asked you to think on your soul's need,
Matins, Mass and evening song;
You must first do other deeds,
You said all was [an] empty affair.
To woods and water and field you went,
Or to court to do men wrong;
Except for pride or greater rewards
Little did you of good among [people].

"Who may do more treason,
Or his lord better displease,
Than he who is towards all his confidences
In and out as he possesses a servant?
Ever since you were thriven and bold,
I acted with all my might,
To provide thee rest and quiet,
And you bring me into pain.

"Now the wild beasts are able to run
And lie under the linden tree and [its] leaf,
And the fowls fly through the fields and fens,

Since thy false heart split.
Thine eyes are blind and cannot know,
    The mouth is dumb, thine ears are deaf;
And now so loathfully you lie grinning,
    From thee comes a wicked smell.

"There is no lady bright of complexion,
    Who was not well wont to think of thee,
Who would lie one night with thee
    For anything that men might give her.
You are unseemly for to see
    Uncomely for to kiss sweetly;
You have no friend that would not flee,
    [If] you [should] come rushing into the street."

The body it said, "I say,
    Ghost, you certainly have pressed
To place all the guilt on me,
    That you have lost thy great happiness.
Where was I by wood or way,
    Sat or stood or did anything badly,
That I was not ever under thy eye?
    Well you know that it is true.

"Whether I went up or down,
    That I bore thee not on my back,
As thine ass from town to town,
    Yet you let me have blows and beatings?
That you were not [present] and directed the conver-
        sation,
    Never did I speak a thing;
Here men might see the truth
    In me that lies so livid and black.

"For all the while you were my companion
   I had all that was needed for myself,
I might speak, see and hear
   I went and rode and drank and ate.
Loathsomely changed is my countenance
   Since the time that you left me;
Deaf and dumb I lie on the bier
   So that I might not stir hand nor foot.

"I should have been dumb as a sheep
   Or as a ewe or as a swine
That ate and drank and lay and sleep,
   Slain and all his pain is passed;
[I should have] never taken heed of property,
   Nor knew what was water or wine,
Nor reclined in Hell that is so deep,
   Were it not for the intelligence that was all thine."

The ghost it said, "[There] is no doubt;
   Body, you bore me about;
You must need [have done it]. I was without
   Hand or foot, I was well aware.
Except as you carried me about,
   I might not do the least piece of work;
Therefore I must need bow the head,
   As does [that one] who dares no other [thing].

"Of one woman born and bred,
   Body, were we both two;
Together fostered fair and fed
   Until you were able to speak and go.
Softly I led thee with love,
   I never dared to do thee harm;

To lose thee I dreaded so sorely,
  And well I knew to get no more.

"For me you would do somewhat
  For a little space of time while you were young,
Because of the eyes of friends who stood by thee,
  The time you were beaten and bruised;
But when you were thriven and strong,
  And knew hunger, cold and thirst,
And what was ease, rest and quiet,
  Thou did all thy own will.

"I saw thee fair of flesh and blood
  And all my love on thee I cast;
That you thrived, I thought good,
  And let thee have rest and quiet.
That made thee so stern of mind,
  And of works so weak;
To fight with thee was of no use
  For you carried me in thy breast.

"Gluttony and lechery,
  Pride and wicked covetousness,
Contention and malice and envy
  To God in Heaven and all His
And in displeasure for to lie,
  Was thy habit in every way;
That I shall now pay for full dearly,
  Alas, indeed, sorely may I fear.

"You were warned before this,
  What we both should have;
Idle tales you held that, though

You saw many down in the grave.
You did all that the world asked of thee,
   And that thy flesh would crave of thee;
I endured thee and did so angrily,
   To be master and I [became] thy servant."

"Know thou, ghost, anything gained by thee
   In order to requite thyself withal,
You who was wrought so worthily,
   To say I made thee my slave?
I never did anything in life,
   I never plundered nor [did] I steal
That first from thee came not the thought;
   Who shall pay, pays it!

"What knew I what was wrong and right,
   What to take or what to avoid,
Except what you put in my sight
   That should know all the wisdom?
When you taught me one evil,
   And began to complain to me thereof,
Then I acted with all my might
   To have my way another time.

"But had you, that Christ granted it,
   Given me hunger, thirst and cold,—
And you blame me who knew no good,—
   When I was so bold in evil;
What I had undertaken in youth
   I have held when I was old;
You let me wander north and south
   And had in [your] power all my will.

"You should for no life nor land,
  Nor for any other gain in the world,
Have allowed me to lay aside [your] hand,
  That has turned to shame and sin
But because I found thee so easy,
  And thy wretched intelligence so thin,
That ever was twisted as a rod,
  Therefore I could never cease.

"To sin you knew was my nature,
  As mankind's it is also,
And of the wretched world so mindful,
  And of the fiend that is our foe.
You should have thought to fetter me before
  When I did wrong and did myself woe;
But when the blind leads the blind
  Into a ditch they, the two, both fall."

Then began the ghost to weep,
  And said, "Body, alas, alas,
That I love thee ever yet,
  For all my love I placed in thee.
That you loved me, you allow,
  And made me a cap of glass;
I did all that was pleasing to thee,
  And you were ever my traitor.

"The fiend of Hell who has envy
  For mankind and ever has had,
Was in us as is a spy,
  When I asked thee to do some good.
The world he took to company,
  Which has deceived many a soul;

They, the three, knew thy folly,
  And made thee, wretch, all mad.

"When I asked thee to take a rest,
  Forsake sin ever and at once,
Do penance, fast and watch,
  The fiend said, 'You shall not so,'
Thus soon [you] forsake all thy happiness
  To live ever in pain and woe!
Joy and happiness I advised you make
  And think to live more years.

"When I asked thee to leave pride,
  Thy many feasts, thy rich dress,
The false world that stood besides,
  Bade thee to be very gay and proud;
To cloth thy flesh with rich robes,
  Not as a beggar in a rag,
And to ride on a high horse
  With much retainers in and out.

"When I asked thee to rise early,
  To take from me thy soul's keep,
You said you might in no way
  Forego the merry morning's sleep.
When you had made your compact
  With the three traitors, sorely I wept;
Ye led me with your cleverness,
  As the butcher does the sheep.

"When the three traitors in a case
  Together were sworn against me,
You all made idle talk
  As I have said before.

You led me through down and dale
    As an ox by the horn,
To there, as the harm is prepared for him,
    Where his throat shall be cut.

"Because of love, I followed all thy will,
    And to my own death, I drew
To follow thee who was my slave,
    That ever was false and fickle;
You did it and I conceded,
    We knew well it was wrong;
Therefore we must keep our ruin,
    Pain and shame and sorrow enough.

"Though all the men now under the moon
    Were set upon a bench to judge
The shames that should be done to us,
    [They] should not conceive half a part.
Nor help us by prayer nor boon,
    Nor may tear us apart with any deceit;
The hellhounds come now soon
    Therefore we must not flinch."

When the body saw the ghost
    Make that moan and all that sorrow,
It said, "Alas, that my life has lasted,
    That I have lived for sin's sake,
That my heart had not burst asunder,
    When I was taken from my mother;
I might have been cast into the earth,
    And laid and rotted in a lake.

"Then I had never learned
    What was evil, nor what was good,

Nor desired anything wrongly,
  Nor suffer pain as I must,
Where no saint might bear our petition
  To Him who bought us with His blood,
When we are burning in Hell,
  To do us good with some mercy."

"Nay, body, nay, now it is too late
  For to pray and to preach,
Now the wagon is at the gate,
  And thy tongue has put away its speech.
To abolish one point of our pain
  [There] is not a physician in the world.
All together we go to the gate,
  Such is God's harsh vengeance.

"But had you a little before,
  While life was lent to us together,
When that [we] were so sick and sear,
  Shriven ourselves and the devil injured,
And let run a sad tear,
  And promised amendment,
[There] was no need for us to have fright or fear
  That God would not have sent us happiness.

"Though all the men that are alive
  Were priests in order to sing Masses,
And all the maidens and the wives
  Widows in order to wring their hands,
And might five [times] such
  As are in this world of all things,
Since we may not shrive ourselves,
  Should not bring us into bliss.

"Body, I may no more dwell,
   Nor stand in order to speak with thee;
I hear the hellhounds yell,
   And fiends more than men might see
That come to fetch me to Hell,
   Nor may I flee from them anywhere;
And you shall come with flesh and skin
   At Judgment Day to live with me."

It [the ghost] had now not ere said the words,
   It knew not whither it should go;
Broke in at a bound
   A thousand devils and more.
When they had laid on him
   With all their sharp clutches then,
It [the ghost] was in a sorry plight,
   Pitifully pulled about to and fro.

Because they were shaggy, rough and tailed,
   With broad humps on their backs;
Sharp claws, long nailed,
   There was no limb without deformity.
On all sides it was attacked
   By many a devil foul and black;
Crying for mercy availed little
   When Christ would punish it so harshly.

Some tore the jaws of it asunder
   And poured in lead so hot,
And commanded him to drink fast,
   And poured [it] about him profusely.
A devil came there at the last
   That was the master, well I know;

A glowing colter he pressed into him
So that it went through his heart.

Some sent glowing swords
Into back and breast and both sides,
So that in his heart the points met,
And made in him then wide wounds,
And they allowed him to see full well
The heart that was so full of pride;
Indeed he had it as men [had] promised him
For it should happen more.

Valuable clothing for to wear
They saw that he loved best;
A devil's cope for to bear,
All burning was cast on him,
With hot clasps made to fasten
That closely sat to back and breast;
A helmet that was little to praise
Came to him and a horse all ready.

Forth was brought therewith a bridle,
A cursed devil as a colt,
That grinned horribly and yawned widely,
The flame it shined from the throat;
With a saddle in the middle of the side
Full of sharp spikes shot,
Also a hatchel to ride on;
All was glowing like a groat.

Upon the saddle he was flung,
As he should [be] in a tournament;
One hundred devils beat on him
Here and there when he was caught;

With hot spears through was [he] stung,
   And with awls all torn asunder;
At the same stroke, the sparks sprang
   As from a brand that was burnt up.

When he who rode had ridden
   Upon the saddle where he sat,
He was cast down as a toad,
   And hellhounds were allowed at him
That then wrenched out large pieces,
   As he was fetched towards Hell;
There all the fiends treaded it underfoot,
   Men might follow the track by the blood.

They bade him to hunt and to blow
   To cry to Bauston and Bewis,
The hunting days that were accustomed for him to know
   He should blow the prize;
A hundred devils in a row,
   Drew him with strings contrary to his wish,
Until they came to that loathsome cave
   Where Hell was, I know, too, certainly.

When it came to that wicked place,
   The fiends cast such a yell,
The earth it opened at once,
   Smoke and dense smoke up it welled;
Both of pitch and of brimstone,
   Men might have the smell five miles away.
Lord, woe shall be possessed by him
   Who has thereof a tenth part!

When the ghost beheld the truth,
   Whither it should [go], it cast a cry

And said, "Jesus, who sits on high,
  On me, thy creature, now have mercy.
Did thou who are so skillful not create me?
  Thy creature also was I
As men that sit so near to Thee,
  That You have done so well by.

"You who knew all beforehand,
  Why did Thou create me to evil fate,
To be thus tugged and torn to pieces,
  And others to have all my weal?
Then [them] who should be lost,
  Wretches, that You might spare,
Alas! woe! why did You permit them to be born
  To give the foul fiend so many?"

Again the fiends began to cry at him,
  "Caitiff, [it] helps thee no more
To call on Jesus and Mary,
  Nor to cry for Christ's grace.
You have lost their company,
  You have served us for so long;
Therefore now you shall abide
  As others that believe in our lore."

The foul fiends that were glad,
  With their heads and tails, they slung at him,
And cast him with might and main
  Down into the devil's pit,
Where the sun shall never be seen;
  He himself sank in therewith;
The earth it locked itself again,
  At once the dungeon it was shut up.

When it was [gone] forth, that foul journey,
  To the abyss of Hell, before it was day,
On each one hair stood a drop
  From fright and fear there as I lay;
To Jesus Christ with mild courage
  Earnestly I called and ever looked,
When those fiends, hot and mad,
  Came to fetch me away.

I thank Him who suffered death,
  For His many mercies and His grace,
That shield me from many a evil,
  As I lay there a sinful man.
Then I, all sinful, advise them with this advice
  To confess themselves and repent sorely;
Never was so great a sin done
  That Christ's mercy is not indeed more.

ADAM AND EVE

Eve has led Seth
To Paradise as Adam bade.
And Eve drew herself from the gate,
She dares not look at anything therein,
She dares not show God her face,
But lets Seth wait for grace.
And Seth in that place,
Sorely weeping, in holy prayer,
He waited there all still,
For God's mercy and God's will.
   Through the virtue of God's might
There came down an angel bright
And said to Seth in this manner,
What he must hear with [his] ears:
"God who has created all the world
Sends the word, you ask for nothing,
Before is gone the period
Of five thousand winters and one,
And five and twenty winters and more.
Before that period is gone,
And God who is full of might
Be alight on the earth,
And have taken the nature of man,
And bathed in the river Jordan;
Then shall Adam and Eve, his wife,
Be anointed with the oil of life,
And all those who come after them
Who have taken Christendom.
Go tell Adam thy father this,

That no other grace is there;
And bid him to hasten to prepare himself,
His time draws near that he shall die.
And when the body that has done sin,
And the soul shall part asunder,
Exactly when that time shall be,
Much wonders shall you see.
So says my Lord that has created all,
And bids that you dread nothing
For nothing that you should hear or see;
So He sent you word by me."

Eve and Seth took their way,
And went again as they came,
And told Adam the message,
That the Heavenly King sent him;
And Adam held up both his hands,
And thanked God for all His message.
Adam opened his eyes,
And afterward he saw his son
And said, "Mercy, sweet Jesus,
Who has wounded my son thus?"

"By God, Adam," said Eve,
"He who is about to injure
Our souls both night and day,
As much as ever he may,
That is the fiend that is our foe,
That has brought us into this woe!
He came and met with us two
As we went on our way
And went towards Paradise;
Thus he bit him in the face."
"Oh, woe, Eve," said Adam then,
"You have wrought much trouble!

All that are born after us,
All shall curse us therefore;
And all that live after us,
Both in the morning and in the evening,
Shall be busy to bear the woe
That is born of us two.
Therefore, Eve, tell all thine children,
Both the young and the old,
That they are filled with our sin,
And bid each one of them begin
To cry for mercy, night and day.
My time has come, I shall die."

Thus Adam asked Eve, his wife,
To teach his children after his life,
How they should begin at once
To cry for mercy for their sins.

And when he had taught them thus,
As the book tells us,
He knelt down in his prayer,
And died at once in that place.
And as the angel had said,
All the brightness was banished;
The sun and the moon lost their light
For six days and six nights.

Eve began to weep and cry,
When she saw Adam die;
And Seth made a sorrowful moan,
And fell down on his father at once,
And as it tells in the book
In his arms he took his father,
And very bitterly he wept.
And God Almighty took notice thereof,
And sent down an angel bright

Who said to Seth right at once,
"Arise, and let thy sorrow be,
And with thine eyes you shall see
God, who shall gladden all the world,
With what He shall do with what He made."
   God who sits in high Heaven
Took Adam's soul so that Seth saw it,
And betook it to Saint Michael
And said: "See after this soul well, take
And put it in sorrow and darkness,
Out of joy and all lightness,
Until five thousand winters have passed,
Two hundred and eight and twenty more,
From the time that he ate
Of the apple he thought so sweet.
So long for his guilt,
In his keeping shall he be pushed,
That made him break my command;
So long will I be avenged
On him and all his blood also,
Because he broke my commandment.
And when that time is passed,
All his woe shall turn to joy;
And afterwards shall he then
Sit in that self same seat
That Lucifer sat, my angel bright,
Before pride was alight in his heart."
   Thus said Jesus who sits on high,
And afterwards He ascended into Heaven.
From the time that the circumstances happened
That cursed Cain slew Abel,
Until Adam died upon the earth,
As sweet Jesus Christ desired it,

Yet Abel lay above the ground;
Until Jesus Christ—He must be heard—
Bade His angel that they should
Bury the body under the ground.

   The angels all without strife
Did at once God's order.
Into clothes they enwrapped the body;
Eve and her children stood and looked on
Right in that self same place,
And had wonders what they the angels did,
For they had not before then
Ever seen any man buried.

   Then the angel said where he stood.
To Eve and to all her brood:
"Take care how we do it,
And here afterwards do thus.
Bury all so, who die
As you see with your eyes;
What we do to this body here,
Do ye in the same manner."
When the angel had said thus,
They went to sweet Jesus
To Heaven where they were foremost,
And left Eve with her children there.

   Six days after Adam was dead,
God Almighty bade an angel bright
To go to tell Eve, Adam's wife
The time was come for her life.

   When Eve knew she should die,
She called forth her progeny,
Both the young and the old,
Her children and her children's children.
And said that all might hear:

"When I and Adam, my mate,
Broke God's commandment,
At once His wrath was sent
On us and on our progeny;
And therefore you shall cry for mercy,
And both by day and also by night
Do penance with all your might.
And you, Seth, for any thing
I command thee on my blessing
That thy father's life be written,
And mine also, every part,
From the beginning of his life
As he was created and I, his wife,
And how we were filled with sin,
And what sorrow we have lived in,
And in which manner that you saw
Readily with thine eyes
Thy father's soul sent to pain,
Because he broke God's commandment.
Observe all this that you write
As well as you can write it
So that those that are now young children
May see it and their elders
And others that are hereafter born,
How we have wrought here before
That they might take example of us
And satisfy Jesus again."
    When Eve had thus spoken,
And her message laid on Seth,
She knelt down and asked their prayers;
And exactly in that very same place,
That all her kin stood and saw
Where, she died before their eyes.

Right at once as Eve was dead,
Her children took themselves to her advice
And carried her that same day
Into the place where Adam lay,
And buried her in that place,
Exactly as the angels did
Who buried Adam and Abel;
Thereof they took heed very well
And when she was brought into the earth,
They were sorry in their thought,
And wept and made much woe.
When Adam and Eve were gone,
Both in the evening and in the morning,
They wept and made much sorrow.

And at the end of the four days,
Jesus made an angel go
And said where they wept sorely:
"Grieve for six days and no more;
The seventh day rest from your sorrow,
Both in the evening and in the morning.
For God who has created all the world,
And all the world made from nothing,
As He thought it would be best,
The seventh day He took rest.
And another thing surely,
It betokens the day of mercy;
The seventh day was Sunday,
And that day shall be Judgment Day,
And all the souls that have worked well
That day shall be brought to rest."

When the angel had said his message,
That Almighty God had laid on him,
He took his way into Heaven—

They never knew where he went.
   Seth right at once began
With Adam who was the first man,
All together he wrote his life,
As Eve, Adam's wife, had asked,
As tells the Book that is well known,
On stone all the letters he wrote,
For fire nor water upon earth
Should never injure it.
When Seth had written Adam's life,
And Eve's who was Adam's wife,
Right in that very place
Where Adam was wont to say his prayers,
In that place he laid the Book,
As wise men before this have said,
Where Adam was wont to say his prayers,
And left it in that place;
And there it lay all through Noah's flood,
And had nothing but good.
   Long after Noah's flood was gone,
Solomon, the King, then came
Who was heir of David's land;
And Adam's life there he found,
And it was all written on stone,
And damaged not a letter was there.
For all that Solomon could
Think in heart or speak with mouth,
Not one word could he know.
Of all that was there written,
He could not understand one word
That Seth had written in his hand.
And Solomon who was wise
Besought the King of Paradise

That He should for his strength
Send him the light of grace from Heaven
So that he might have the grace to know
What things were written there.

God—He must be blessed—
He sent an angel onto the earth
Who taught Solomon every part,
All of Adam's written life,
And said to Solomon indeed:
"Here, where this writing is,
Exactly in this very spot,
Adam was wont to say his prayers.
And here you shall build a temple
That shall be called a holy Church,
Where men shall say holy prayers
As Adam did in this place."
And Solomon, the King, at once
Thought to build a temple of lime and stone,
The first Church under the sun
That ever in the world was begun.

Now you have heard of Adam's life,
And of Eve who was his wife,
Which life they led here on earth,
And afterwards did as God desired.
And when Adam was dead on the earth,
For sins that came from her seed,
God sent Noah's flood
And drowned all the brood;
Such vengeance God took
On all that came from Adam,
Save Noah and his wife
Whom God had granted life,
And his children that he had

That he led with him on the ship.
  Of Noah and of his children
We all together are come.
And after they lived in such sin
That for the life they lived in,
Sodom and Gomorrah, that were then
Two such noble cities,
Both sank into Hell,
As we hear clerks tell.
And another noble city,
That was called Nineveh,
Was in the same circumstances;
But as the prophet Jonas
Begged for them by day and night
To sweet Jesus full of might,
And made both King and Queen,
And all the other people pray,
In their prayers he made them awake,
And had them take hard penance.
And when they were pushed to penance,
God forgave them their guilt;
Thus Nineveh was saved
Through the imploring of Jonas.
  Yet after Noah's flood
All that came from Noah's blood,—
Were he never so holy a man,—
For the sin that Adam began,
There, none must come into Heaven,
Before God had taken His counsel
To alight in the Virgin Mary,
And on the cross would die,
In order to purchase us all free,—
Heard and exalted must He be.

Now have ye heard of sweet Jesus,
As the Book tells us;
Of the world how it began,
And how He made man from earth.
Jesus who was taken wrongly,
And suffered many strong pains
Among the Jews who were cruel,
To bring Adam out of Hell,
Give us grace in order to win
The joy that Adam now is in.

HAVELOK THE DANE

In that time as it happened,
Was in the land of Denmark
A rich King and very strong;
The name of him was Birabein.
He had many knights and servants;
He was a fair man and valiant,
Of body he was the best knight
That might ever lead an army out,
Or ride on steed, or handle a spear.
Three children he had by his wife,
He loved them as his life;
He had a son and daughters two,
Very fair as it happened.
He that will not spare,
Rich nor poor, King nor emperor,
Death took him when he would best
Live; but his days were filled,
So that he might not live any more,—
For gold nor silver nor for any gift.
    When he knew that, he quickly sent
After priests far and near,
Good Canons and monks also,
In order to guide and to advise him;
In order to administer the Eucharist and to shrive him,
While his body was alive.
When he received communion and confessed,
His will made and given for him,
He did [make] all his knights sit down,
For through them he desired to know

Who might care for his young children,
Until that they could speak with tongue;
Spoke, went, and rode on horse,
Knights and servants by their side.
He spoke thereof and soon chose
A rich man that under the moon
Was the truest that he knew,
Godard, the King's own friend;
And said that he might look after them best,
If that he undertook them
Until his son might bear
Helmet on his head and lead an army out,
In his hand a strong spear,
And be made King of Denmark.
He believed well what he said,
And on Godard laid his hands
And said, "Here I deliver to thee
Mine children all three,
All Denmark and all my property,
Until my son be of age.
But that I will, that you swear
On the altar, and on the Mass garments,
On the bells that men ring,
On the Massbook the priest sings in,
That you shall care for my children well,
That their kin be very well agreeable,
Until my son might be a knight,
Then deliver to him his kingdom then,
Denmark and what belongs thereto,
Castles and towns, woods and plains."
Godard stirred up and swore all that
The King asked him and after sat
By the knights who were there,
Who wept all very sorely

For the King who died soon.
Jesus Christ who made the moon
To shine in the murky night,
Kept his soul from the pains of Hell,
And allowed that it might live
In the heavenly kingdom with God's Son.
　　When Birabein was laid in the grave,
The earl soon did take the boy,
Havelok, who was the heir,
Swanborow, his sister, Helfled the other,
And in the castle did he put them
Where no one might come to them
Of their kin, where they were fastened.
There they wept very sorely,
Both because of hunger and because of the cold,
Before they were three winters old.
Scarcely he gave them clothing,—
He gave not a nut for his oaths;
He clothed them [not] rightly, nor fed them
Nor put them to bed richly.
Then was Godard certainly
Under God the most wicked
Who ever was created on earth,
Except one, the wicked Judas.
Have he the malediction today
Of all that ever may speak!
Of patriarch and of pope
And of priest with locking cope;
Also of monks and hermits,
And of the dear Holy Cross
On which ran the blood of God Himself!
[May] Christ condemn him with His mouth;
He was condemned in North and South
By all men who could speak,

By Christ who made the moon and sun!
　When he had in all the land
All the people enticed into his hands,
And all had sworn oaths to him,
Rich and poor, the dear and the loathed,
That they should do his will,
And that they should not irritate him,
He thought of a very strong treachery,
A treason and a felony,
For to make for the children,—
The devil of Hell take him soon!
When that was thought, he went at once
To the tower where they were fastened,
Where they wept for hunger and cold.
The boy who was somewhat bold,
Came again to him, knelt down [before] him,
And to Godard, very fair he there wept.
And Godard said, "What is [the matter] with you?
Why weep ye and howl now?"
　"For we are very sorely hungry."
He said without more;
"We have not [food] to eat, we have not
Herein either knight or boy
Who gives us drink or food
Half a part that we might eat.
Woe are we that we were born!
Woe, alas, is there no corn
That men might make bread with?
We are hungry, we are nearly dead."
　Godard heard their woe,—
Thereof he gave not a straw,—
But took the maidens both together,
Also it was according to his jest,
Also he would play with them,

Who were green and pale because of hunger.
Of both, he carved their throats in two,
And after carved them all to pieces.
There was sorrow, [for] whosoever saw it,
When the children by the wall
Lay and sprawled in their blood.
Havelok saw it and there stood by.
Very sorry was that good boy,
Much dread he must have [had,]
For at his heart he saw a knife
In order to rob him of his life.
But the boy who was small,
He knelt before that Judas,
And said, "Lord, mercy now!
Homage, Lord, I give to thee;
All Denmark I will give thee
To that agreement [that] you let me live.
Here I will swear on the Book
That never more shall I bear
Against thee, Lord, shield nor spear,
Nor other weapon that may harm you.
Lord, have mercy on me;
Today I will flee from Denmark,
Never more to come again.
Swear will I that Birabein
Never yet begot me."
    When the devil heard that
Somewhat he began for to repent,
Withdrew the knife that was warm
With the blood of the good children.
There was a miracle fair and good,
That he did not slay the boy,
But for pity, he withdrew.
Of Havelok he repented full sorely,

And thought that he [Godard] desired that he [Havelok]
    were dead,
But that he [might] not with his own hands
Kill him, that foul fiend;
Thought he as he stood by him
Staring as he were mad,
"If I let him go alive,
He might work me much woe;
Peace, I have not any more,
He may wait in order to slay me.
And if he were brought from life,
And my children would thrive,
Lordings after me
Of all Denmark they might be.
[May] God know it, he shall be dead,
I will take no other advice;
I shall act to cast him into the sea,
Where I desire that he be drowned;
About his neck a good anchor
That he might not float in the flood."
There at once did he send
After a fisherman that he thought
Who would do all his will,
And soon anon he said to him,
"Grim, you know that you are my slave;
Will you do all my will
That I will bid thee,
Tomorrow I shall make thee free,
And give thee property and make [thee] rich.
With that, you will take this child,
And lead him with thee tonight,—
When you see the moonlight,—
And put him therein into the sea,
I will take on me all the sin."

Grim took the child and bound him fast
While the bonds might last,
That were of very strong rope.
Then was Havelok in very great pain;
Never before did he know what woe was.
Jesus Christ who made to go
The lame and the dumb to speak,
Havelok, avenge thee of Godard.

When Grim had him bound fast,
And after wound in an old cloth,
A gag of rags, very foul,
So that he might not speak nor breathe
Where he would bear or lead him,—
When he had done that deed,
When the deceiver had asked him
That he should lead him forth
And drown him in the sea,—
That agreement made he,—
In a bag, full and black,
He soon cast him on his back
And carried him home to his house;
And took him to Dame Leve
And said, "Guard you this boy
Wholly, so you might possess life with me.
I shall drown him in the sea;
Because of him we shall be made free,
Have gold enough and other property;
That my lord has promised me."

When Dame Leve heard that,
Up she stirred and sat not,
And cast the boy adown so hard
That he there cracked his crown
Against a great stone where it lay;

Then was Havelok able to say, "Woe, alas,
That ever I was born of Kings!"
Who has not for himself a raven or eagle,
Lion, or wolf, wolverine or bear,
Or other beast that would protect him.
So lay that child until midnight
That Grim bade Leve bring a light
In order to put on his clothes:
"Think you not of mine oaths
That I have sworn to my lord?
I will not be lost;
I shall carry him to the sea,
You know that it profits me,
And I shall drown him therein;
Rise up quickly and go thou within,
And blow the fire and light a candle."

As she should handle his clothes
In order to put [them] on and blow the fire,
She saw therein a very bright light,
All so bright as it were day
About the boy where he lay.
Out of his mouth there stood a vapor,
As it were a sunbeam;
Also was there a light therein,
As there burnt wax candles in[side.]
"Jesus Christ!" Said Dame Leve,
"What is that light in our House.
Rise up, Grim, and see what it means,
What is the light as you think?"
They both stirred up to the boy,—
For man shall have good will,—
Ungagged him and unbound [him] quickly,
And soon at once found upon him,

As they turned out his shirt,
On his right shoulder a royal mark,
All very bright, all very fair.
   "God knows," said Grim, "This is our heir
Who shall be lord of Denmark;
He shall be King strong and stark,
He shall have in his hand
All Denmark and England.
He shall do Godard much harm,
He shall hang him or quickly flay,
Or he shall bury him all quickly,
On him, he shall have no mercy."
Thus said Grim and wept sorely,
And soon fell he to his feet,
And said, "Lord, have mercy
On me and Leve who is with me!
Lord, we are both thine,
Thine churls, thine servants.
Lord, we will feed thee well,
Until that you can ride a steed,
Until that you can carry very well
A helmet on [your] head, a shield and a spear;
Never shall know certainly,
Godard, that foul traitor.
Through other man, Lord, than through thee
Shall I never a freeman be.
You shall, Lord, make me free,
For I shall care for thee and watch [thee;]
Through thee I shall have freedom."
   Then was Havelok a glad boy;
He sat himself up and craved for bread
And said, "I am nearly dead,
What for hunger, what for bonds,

That you laid on my hands,
And for the gag at the last,
That in my mouth was thrust fast;
I was therewith so hard fettered
That I was therewith nearly strangled."

"[It] is well with me that you might eat;
God knows," said Leve, "I shall feed thee.
Bread and cheese, butter and milk,
Pastries and pancakes, with all such [things]
Shall we soon feed thee well,
Lord, in this great need;
True it is that men said and swear,
Where God will keep, nothing harms."

When she had brought the food,
Havelok at once began to eat
Ravenously and was very glad;
He could not conceal his hunger.
A loaf he ate and more, I know,
For he was very sorely hungry.
Three days before this [time], I know,
He ate no food, that was well seen.
When he had eaten and was fed,
Grim did make a very fair bed;
Unclothed him and put him therein,
And said, "Sleep, son, with much pleasure,
Sleep well fast and dread thee nothing,
From sorrow to joy art thou brought."

Soon as it was light of day,
Grim he undertook his way
To the wicked traitor, Godard,
Who was the steward of Denmark,
And said, "Lord, I have done
What you asked me with the boy;

He is drowned in the flood,
About his neck a good anchor.
He is evidently dead,
Never more eats he bread;
He lies drowned in the sea:—
Give me gold and other property,
That I might be rich,
And with thy charter make me free,
For you very well promised it to me
When I last spoke with thee."
Godard stood and looked at him
Thoroughly with grim eyes,
And said, "Will you now be an earl?
Go home quickly, foul dirty churl;
Go heathen and be evermore
Slave and churl, as you were before;
You shall have no other reward.
For little, I shall lead thee to put [thee]
On the gallows as God advises me,
For you have done a wicked deed.
You might stand here for a long [time,]
But you [will] go [away] a very heathen."
   Grim thought to leave so that he ran
From that traitor, that wicked man,
And thought, "What shall I [do] for advice?
[If he] knew him alive, he would both of us
Hang high on the gallowtree.
Better for us is to flee from the land,
And protect both our lives,
My children and my wife's."
Grim soon sold all his corn,
Sheep with wool, cattle with horns,
Horses and swine and goats with beards,

The geese, the hens of the yard,—
He sold all that availed anything,
That he ever might sell,
And he drew all to the penny.
His ship he prepared well enough;
He did cover it with tar and very well with pitch
That it feared not sand nor creek;
Thereon he put a very good mast,
Strong and very firm cables,
Good oars, and a very good sail;
Therein wanted not a nail
That ever he should put therein.

When he had prepared it so,
Havelok the young he put therein,
Himself and his wife, his three sons,
And his two daughters who were fair;
And soon did he lean on the oar,
And drew himself to the high seas,
Where he might flee best of all.
From land were they but a mile,
There was never but any time
That there not began to rise a wind
Out of the North, men call bise [the Northwind,]
And drove them to England,
That was afterwards all in his hands,
His, that Havelok, was the name;
But before he had much shame,
Much sorrow and much injury;
And afterwards he got it all together,
As you shall now forthwith learn,
If that you will hear it thereto.

In Humber, Grim began to land,
At Lindsley exactly at the north end;

There sat his ship upon the sand,
But Grim drew it up to the land.
And there he made a little cottage
For himself and all his company;
He began there for to dwell
To make a little house of earth,
So that he was there well
Sheltered by their harbor there:
And for that Grim who owned the place,
The name of Grim caught on to the place
So that Grimsby, [all do] call it
That thereof all speak,
And so shall men call it ever
Between this [time] and doomsday.

ROBERT MANNING'S HANDLYNGE SYNNE

The Tale of Pierce the Usurer

Usurers and money lenders,
They are as wicked as Saracens.
Whosoever might prove which they were,
Were they unlearned or were they learned;
They shall not come into Christ's flock,
Nor come into the Church, nor the Churchyard.
Nonetheless by this skill
They might be saved, if that they will
Leave that sin and do [it] no more,
And do the teachings of Holy Church;
And give back that same thing
That they have taken in usury;
If they might not give it back,
[They might] help the poor men therewith to live
Charitably and with good will,
And they might balance their ill deeds.
A good example might ye hear,
Of Pierce who was a toll collector;
And I shall tell you as quickly
How he was both good and bad.
Saint John, the almoner
Said [that] Pierce was a usurer,
And was very covetous,
And a niggard and avaricious,
And gathered pennies into a treasure
As usurers do everywhere.
  It happened thus upon a day

That poor men sat along the way,
And spread their hatred in their bosoms
Against the sun that was warm,
And told the custom houses to each one
By which they had [done] good and at which no;
Where they had [done] well, they praised well,
And where they had [received] naught, not a deal.
As they spoke of many things,
Pierce came forth to that gate;
Then said each one who sat or stood,
"Here comes Pierce who never did good."
Each one said to the other chattering,
They never took good from Pierce's hand;
Nor shall poor men ever have any.
Could he never so well crave.
One of them began to say,
"A wager dare I with you lay
That I shall have some good from him,
Be he never so harsh nor cruel."
To that wager they all assented
To give him a gift, if it might happen so.
    This man started up and took his way
Until he came to Pierce's gate.
As he stood still and waited for the evil one,
One came with an ass loaded with bread;
That same bread Pierce had bought,
And to his house should it be brought.
When he saw Pierce come there withal,
The poor man thought, now shall I ask:
"I ask thee for some good for charity,
Pierce, if [it] be thy will."
Pierce stood and looked at him
Felonously with grim eyes.

He stooped down to find a stone,
But as fortune was, he then found none.
For the stone, he took a loaf,
And at the poor man threw it.
   The poor man grabbed it up quickly,
And was thereof very wonderfully happy.
To his fellows fast he ran
With the loaf, this poor man.
"Lo," he said, "what I have,
A gift from Pierce, so God save me."
"Nay," swore they by their prosperity,
"Pierce never gave such a gift."
He said, "You should well understand
That I had it from Pierce's hand;
That I dare swear on the sacraments
Here before each of you."
Great wonder had they all
That such a chance might happen to him.
   The third day,—thus is it written,—
Pierce fell into a great sickness;
And as he lay in his bed,
He thought indeed that he was led
With one who was sent after him
To come into his judgment.
Before the judge was he brought
To give account how he had wrought.
Pierce stood very sorely afraid,
And was abashed as insane;
He saw a fiend on the one side
Accusing him very evilly.
All of it was showed before him
How he had lived since he was born,
And namely every wicked deed

Since first he could lead himself
Why he did them and for what motive,
For all it behooved him to give a reason.
On the other side stood men very bright
Who would have saved him with their might,
But they might find no good,
That might save or unbind him.
The fair men said, "What is to explain?
We find no good deed in him
By which God is paid except a loaf
The which Pierce threw at the poor man.
Yet he gave it with no good will,
But cast it after him with ill;
For God's love he gave it not,
Nor for almsgiving had he thought it.
Nonetheless, the poor man
Had the loaf from Pierce then."
The fiend had laid in balance
His wicked deeds and his mischances;
They laid the loaf against his deeds,—
They had nothing else they might need,—
The holy man tells us and says
That the loaf made even weight.
Then said these fair men to Pierce,
"If you be wise, now you learn
How this loaf helped thee in need
To aid thy soul with almsgiving."
Pierce began to awake from his sleep,
And began to think greatly about his dream,
Sighing with a mourning countenance
As a man who was in great doubt,
How that he was accused
By many fiends for his trespasses,

And how they would have damned him there,
If [it] were not for the mercy of Jesus Christ.
All this he cast in his heart,
And to himself he spoke at last,
That "For a loaf in evil will
Helped me in so great a peril,
Much would it help in need
To do almsgiving with a good will."
From that time then Pierce grew [into]
A man of such fair manners,
That no one might find in him
But a man both meek and kind to the poor;
A milder man might not be,
Nor to the poor more with alms free,
And sorrowful of heart also was he
That you might learn here in this passage.

    Pierce met upon a day
A poor man by the way
As naked as he was born,
Who had lost all in the sea.
He came to Pierce where he stood
And asked him for some of his goods,
Somewhat of his clothing,
For the love of the King of Heaven.
Pierce was of sorrowful heart,
He took his kirtle off very quickly
And put it on the man [mentioned] above,
And bade him wear it for His love.
The man took it and was very happy;
He went and sold it very quickly.

    Pierce stood and did behold
How the man sold the kirtle,
And was therewith fearfully mad

That he sold so soon his clothes.
He might no longer for sorrow stand,
But went home very sorely weeping,
And said it was an evil sign,
And that [he] himself was not worthy
To be in his prayers;
Therefore he [the man] would not wear the kirtle.
   When he had wept very long,
And partly therefrom began to leave off,—
For commonly after weeping
Men fall soon into sleep,—
As Pierce lay in his sleep,
He thought a fair dream.
He thought he was alight in Heaven,
And of God he had a sight,
Sitting in his kirtle clad,
That the poor man from him had;
And spoke to him very mildly,
"Why weepest thou and art sorry?
Lo, Pierce," He said, "This is thy cloth;
Because he sold it, you were angry;
Know it well, if you can,
For Me you gave it to the poor man;
That you gave [it] to him in charity,
Every bit you gave it to Me."
   Pierce moved out of sleep,
And thought in great wonder and after said,
"Blessed be all poor men
For God Almighty loves them;
And well are they that are poor here,
They are to God both loved and dear,
And I shall try by night and day
To be poor if that I may."

Hastily he took his property
And gave to the poor men each part.
 Pierce called his clerk to him
That was his notary and bade him listen:—
"I shall show you in secret,
A thing that you can do for me,
I desire that you tell it to no man;
My body I take here for thee to sell
To some man as in bondage,
To live in poverty and in servitude;
Except you do this, I will be angry,
And you and thine shall be loath to me.
If you do it, I shall give thee
Ten pounds of gold to live well with;
The ten pounds I give thee here
And sell me in the manner of a bondsman,
I care not unto whom,
Except only he have Christianity.
The ransom that you shall take for me,
Therefore you shall make security
In order to give it happily and well
To poor men every part,
And withhold thereof no thing,
[Not even] the amount of a farthing."
 His clerk was in woe to do this deed,
But [did it] only because of menace and because of dread.
Because of dread, Pierce made him do it,
And made him plight his troth thereto.
When his clerk had made his oath,
Pierce put on himself a dirty garment;
Unto a Church they both went
In order to fulfill his will in deed.
When that they had come to the Church,

"Lord," thought the clerk, "now whom
Might I find on this same occasion,
To whom I might sell Pierce well?"
    The clerk looked everywhere,
And at the last he knew where
A rich man was that before had been
Ever among special knowledge
But through mischance, on an occasion,
All his goods were lost;
Yule, thus was that man called,
And knew the clerk well by sight.
They spoke of old acquaintances,
And Yule told him of his fortune.
"Yes," said the clerk, "I advise you buy
A man to do thy merchandise,
Whom you may hold in servitude
To restore well thy losses."
    Then said Yule, "In such trade
Would I fain spend my silver."
    The clerk said, "Lo, here [is] one,
A true man and a gentle [one,]
Who will serve thee to satisfaction,
Carefully in all that he may.
Pierce shall you call his name,
Because of him you shall much profit.
He is a very gracious man
To win goods into thy house,
And God shall give thee his blessing,
And success in all things."
    The clerk gave all his ransom
To the poor men of the town,—
Fully all that he took,
He withheld not the value of a farthing.—

The Emperor sent his messengers
All about in order to seek Pierce,
But they might never hear
Of rich Pierce, the toll-collector,
In what place he was taken,
Nor whitherward [what] he was become;
Neither would the clerk tell anyone
Whitherward that Pierce was gone.

   Now is Pierce become useful,
Who was before stout and rich.
All that any man asked him,
Pierce did it with a glad heart.
He grew so mild and so meek,
A milder man no one thought to seek;
For he had made himself meek beyond reason
In order to wash pots and dishes.
To great penance he began to take himself,
And much for to fast and watch,
And he loved patience much
To rich, to poor, to more, to less.
Of all men he would have fear
And bow to their bidding meekly;
Would they ask him to sit or to stand,
Ever he would be obedient.
And since he bore himself so meekly and softly,
Evil persons very often mistreated him,
And held him [to be] foolish or mad,
For he was so mild of manner.
And they that were his fellows
Slandered him most in their talks;
And he suffered all their upbraiding,
And never said anything against them.

   Yule, his lord, well understood

That all his grace and all his goods
Came to him because of the love of Pierce,
Who was of so holy a manner.
And when he knew of his bounty,
He called Pierce [to him] in private:
"Pierce," he said, "you are worthy
For to be honored more than I,
For you are well with Jesus,
He shows great favor for you;
Therefore I shall make thee free,
I desire that you be my fellow."
Thereto Pierce assented not
To be a freeman as he besought;
He desired to be as he was before
In that servitude evermore.
He thanked the lord mildly
For his great courtesy.
  Afterwards Jesus, through His might,
He showed to Pierce a sight,
In order to be strong in his temptation,
And for him to have desire of love.
"Be not sorrowful to do penance,
I am with you in every chance;
Pierce, I, mindful of thee, have,
Here, lo, the kirtle you gave for Me,
Therefore I shall send thee grace
To end well in all goodness."
  [It] happened that sergeants and squires
That were wont to serve Pierce
Went on a pilgrimage, as in case,
To that country where Pierce was.
Yule began to greet them very fairly,
And invited them home to his hall.

Pierce was there [on] that same occasion,
And he knew every one of them well.
He served all of them as a servant
Who was wont to have their service.
But Pierce they recognized not yet,
Because of penance was changed his countenance;
Therefore they beheld him not fast,
And often they cast their eyes on him
And said, "He who stands here
Is like to Pierce, the toll-collector."
He hid his face all that he might
Out of knowledge of their sight;
Nonetheless they beheld him more
And knew him well, all that were there
And said, "Yule, is yonder thy page?
A rich man is in thy servitude;
The Emperor both far and near
Has searched for him whom we find here."

Pierce listened and heard them speaking,
And that they had knowledge of him;
And secretly he took [himself] away
Until he came to the porter.
The porter had lost his speech,
And hearing also since he was born;
But through the grace of sweet Jesus
Was showed fair favor because of Pierce.
Pierce said, "Let me therefore go."
The porter spoke and said, "Yes."
He that was deaf and dumb also,
Spoke when Pierce spoke to him.
Pierce went out the gate,
And went thither where God sent him.

The porter went up to the hall,

And told this miracle to them all,
How the scullion in the kitchen,
Pierce, who had lived herein,
He asked leave right now lately
And went forth out of the gate.
"I advise you all, give good heed,
Whitherward that Pierce is gone;
With Jesus Christ he is secret,
And that is well shown in me.
For what time he spoke to me
Out of his mouth, I thought broke
A flame of fire bright and clear;
The flame made me both speak and hear,
Speak and hear now both I may,
Blessed be God and Pierce today."

    The lord and all the guests,
One and the other that were in the hall,
Had marveled that it was so,
That he might do such miracles.
Then also they quickly sought Pierce,
But all their seeking was for naught.
Pierce they never found,
Night nor day at any time,
For He that took Enoch and Elias
He took Pierce through His mercy,
To lead [him] to rest without end,
Because of his meekness and good deeds.

    Take an example here of Pierce,
And divide [your wealth] with the poor, ye usurers,
For you shall never come to joy within,
But you leave first that sin,
And give in alms that very thing
That you have won through usury.
Now with God we leave Pierce;
God give us grace to follow his ways.

THE WEST MIDLAND PROSE PSALTER

Psalm I

Blessed be the man that goes not in the counsel of the wicked, nor stands in the ways of sinners, nor sits in false judgment. 2. But his will is in the will of Our Lord, and he shall think on His laws both day and night. 3. And he shall be as a tree that is set by the course of waters that shall give its fruit in its time. 4. And his leaves shall not fall, and all things that the rightful do shall multiply. 5. Not so be the wicked, not so; [they be] as a powder that the wind casts from the face of the earth. 6. Therefore shall the wicked not arise in judgment, nor the sinners in the counsel of the rightful. 7. For Our Lord knows the way of the rightful, and the way of the sinners shall perish.

Psalm XXIII

Our Lord governs me, and nothing shall weaken me; In the place of the pastures he sets me there. 2. He nourished me with water for refreshment; He turned my soul from the fiend. 3. He led me up the paths of righteousness for His name. 4. For although I shall have gone amid the shadows of death, I shall fear no evils, for you are with me. 5. Thy discipline and Thy correction comforted me. 6. You made ready grace in my sight against them that troubled me. 7. You make my head fat with mercy; and my drink, making drunk, is very clear. 8. And Thy mercy shall follow me all the days of my life. 9. And that I dwell in the house of Our Lord the length of [my] days.

Psalm XXIV

1. The earth is the Lord's and His plenty; the world and I [are] one that liveth therein. 2. For He built it upon the seas and made it ready upon the rivers. 3. Who shall climb unto the mountain of Our Lord, or who shall stand in His holy place. 4. The innocent in hand and of clean heart that takes his soul not in idleness and swears not in deceit to his neighbor. 5. He shall take the blessing of Our Lord and the mercy of God his help. 6. This is the be-getting of the seeking Him; seeking the face of the God of Jacob. 7. Open your gates, ye princes of Hell, and be ye lifted, ye everlasting gates, and the King of Glory shall enter. 8. Which is He, that King of Glory? The Lord strong and mighty, the Lord mighty in battle. 9. Open your gates, ye princes of Heaven, and be ye lifted, ye ever-lasting gates, and the King of Glory shall enter. 10. Which is He, that King of Glory? The Lord of strength, He is the King of Glory.

Psalm LI

1. Have mercy on me, God, after Thy great mercy. 2. And after the greatness of Thy pity, put away my wickedness. 3. Wash me more from my wickedness and cleanse me of my sin. 4. For I know my wickedness, and my sin is evermore against me. 5. I have sinned to thee alone, and I have done evil before thee, that you be made rightful in thy words, and that you overcome when you are judged. 6. See for I am conceived in wickedness, and my mother conceived me in sins. 7. See, for you love truth; the uncertain things and secret of wisdom you made open to me. 8. You sprinkle me, Lord, with thy mercy, and I shall be made clean; thou shall purify me and I shall be made white as snow. 9. You shall give joy and gladness

to my hearing, and the mild deeds of my heart shall gladden.   10. Turn thy face from my sins, and take away all mine wickedness.   11. Ah, God, make in me a clean heart, and renew thou a right spirit in my heart.   12. Put me not from thy face, and take not away from me thy holy spirit.   13. Give to me the gladness of thy help and strengthen me with thine holy spirit.   14. I shall teach the wicked thine ways, and the wicked shall be converted to thee.   15. Ah, Thou God, God of my health, deliver me from sins, and my tongue shall gladden thy righteousness.   16. Lord, thou shall open my lips, and my mouth shall speak thy praise.   17. For if you had wished, I had given sacrifice; truly you shall not delight in sacrifices.   18. Troubled spirit is sacrifice to God; thou, God, shall not despise the sorrowful and meek heart.   19. Do blissfully, Lord, to thy chosen in thy good will, that the good be strengthened in the heavens.   20. When thou shall take sacrifice of right service and honors; they shall then set goodness before thy throne.

Psalm XC

1. Lord, thou art made succor to us from kind to kind. 2. Before that the mountains were made, or the earth was formed and the world, thou art God from the world unto the world without end.   3. Turn thou nothing into mildness; and you said, ye children of men, turn thou.   4. For a thousand years are before thine eyes as yesterday that is passed.   5. And the keeping one night that had been for nothing, shall be their years.   6. He passes as grass in the morning; flourishes he in the morning and passes; falls he at evening, and hardens and grows he dry.   7. For we fail in thy ire, and we are disturbed in thine vengeance. 8. You layest our wickedness in thy sight; our world is in the illumination of thy face.   9. For all our days faileth,

and we fail in thy wrath.   10. Our years shall appear as
the spider, the days in our years in the seventy years.   11.
Truly if eighty years be in the mighty, the more over them
shall be travail and sorrow.   12. For mildness comes therein, and we shall be taken away.   13. Who knows the power
of thine ire, and to tell thy wrath for thy dread?   14. Make
so thine help known, and the learned of heart in wisdom.
15. Lord, be thou turned unto now, and be thou gracious
with thy servants.   16. We are early fulfilled of thy mercy,
we shall gladden and delight in all our days.   17. We are
glad in the day in which you made us low, for the years
in which we looked after evil.   18. Look to thy servants
and to thine works, and make straight their sons.   19. And
the shining of Our Lord God be with us, and make straight
for us the works of our hands, and make straight for us the
works of our hands.

Psalm XCI

1. He that lives in the help of the highest, he shall dwell
in the defense of God of Heaven.   2. He shall say to Our
Lord, You are my protector and my refuge; my God, I
shall hope in him.   3. For he delivered me from the traps
of the fiends and from the cruel words of men.   4. And
he shall shadow thee with his shoulders, and you shall hope
under his feathers.   5. The truth of him shall encompass
thee with a shield, and you shall not fear of the dread of
night;   6. Of temptation growing in the day, from need
going into darkness, from the curse of the fiend shining
bright.   7. A thousand temptations shall fall from thy side,
and ten thousand from thy right half; the devil, truly, shall
not come to thee.   8. You shall see, truly, with thine eyes,
you shall see the recompense of sinners.   9. For you, Lord,
art mine hope, and you set thy refuge highest of all.   10.
Evil shall not come to thee, and torment shall not come near

to thy tabernacle.   11. For he sent his angel to thee that
they keep thee in thine ways.   12. They shall carry thee in
[their] hands that you are not hurt, perchance, thy spirit
with vices.   13. You shall go according to wisdom and
goodness, and you shall tread under foot the fiend and
Hell.   14. For he hoped in me, and I shall deliver him; I
shall defend him, for he knew my name.   15. He cried to
me, and I shall hear him; I am with him in tribulation, I
shall defend him and glorify him.   16. I shall fill him with
length of days, and I shall show him mine health.

Psalm CIII

1. Ah, thou, my soul, bless Our Lord; and all things that
are within me, bless his holy name.   2. Ah, thou, my soul,
bless Our Lord; and you will never forget all his re-
compenses.   3. The which is merciful to all thine wickedness; the which heals all thy sickness.   4. The which ran-
soms thy life from death; the which crowns thee with
mercies and pities.   5. The which fulfills thy desire in
goods; thy youth shall be made new as an eagle's.   6. Our
Lord is doing mercies and judgment to all thee suffering
wrong.   7. He made his ways known to Moses; he gave
to the children of Israel their wishes.   8. Our Lord is
righteous and merciful, and of long will and greatly merciful.   9. He shall not become angry himself without end,
nor shall he threaten without end.   10. He did nothing to
us after our sins, nor yields he anything to us after our
wickedness.   11. For after the height of Heaven from
earth, he strengthens his mercy to them who fear him.
12. He made far from us our wickedness, as the East departs from the West.   13. As the father has mercy on his
children, Our Lord is merciful to them that fear him; for
he knows our weaknesses.   14. He recorded that we are
powder. Man is as hay; his days are as flowers of the field;

so shall he flourish.   15. For the spirit shall pass from him,
and he shall not live, and he shall know no more his place.
16. The mercy of Our Lord is truly from without end
unto without end to them who fear him.   17. And his
righteousness is unto the children of the children of them
who keep his commands.   18. And they are remembering
of his commandments to do them.   19. Our Lord shall prepare his seat in Heaven and his kingdom shall rule all.
20. Ah, all his angels, mighty of power, doing his word,
to hear the voice of his words, bless Our Lord.   21. Ah,
all his strength, bless Our Lord; you his ministers that do
his will, bless Our Lord.   22. All ye, the works of Our
Lord, bless Our Lord in all places of his lordship; ah, you,
my soul, bless Our Lord.

THE EARL OF TOULOUSE

They all assented to the saw,
They thought he spoke reason and law.
    Then answered the King with the crown,
"Fair [it] happens for thee for thine advice."
He called knights of noble price,
    And bade them be ready to obey
In order to cry throughout all the land,
Both by sea and by sand,
    If they might find
A man who is so much of might,
That for that lady dare take the fight;
    He shall have his treasure.

Messengers, I understand,
Cried throughout the land
    In many a rich city,
If any man dare try his might
In a true quarrel for to fight,
    Well advanced should he be.
The Earl of Toulouse heard of this,
What distress befell the lady,
    Thereof he thought a great pity.
If he knew that she had right,
He would adventure his life to fight
    For that lady free.

For her, he mourned night and day,
And to himself began to say
    He would adventure his life:

"If I may [have] intelligence that she be true,
They that have accused her shall be sorry,
    Except they cease from their strife."
The earl said, "By Saint John,
Into Germany will I go
    Where I have many enemies;
I pray to God full of might,
That I have a true quarrel to fight
    Out of trouble to win that wife."

He rode ahunting on a day,
A merchant met he on the way
    And asked him from whence he was.
"Lord," he said, "from Germany."
At once the earl began to question him
    Of that same case.
"Wherefore is your Empress
Put in so great distress,
    Tell me for the grace of God;
So may thou prosper, Is she guilty?"
"Nay, by Him who died on the tree,
    Who created man after his face."

Then said the earl without hindrance,
"When is the day set,
    That she shall be burnt?"
The merchant said, "Certainly,
This day three weeks even,
    And therefore woe is me."
The earl said, "I thee shall tell,
Good horses I have to sell,
    And steeds two or three.
Certainly might I sell them there,

Thither with thee would I go
   That sight in order to see."

The merchant said with gracious words,
"Into the land, if you will go,
   It would be for your profit;
There may ye sell them at your will."
At once the earl said to him,
   "Sir, hearken to me now;
On this journey will thou remain with me,
Twenty pounds I shall account to thee
   For reward, I make an avowal."
The merchant granted it at once
The earl said, "By Saint John
   Thy will I allow."

The earl told him at that time,
Where he should take himself,
   And homeward went he.
He prepared himself so that no one knew,
For great in him was his trust.
   He said, "Sir, go with me."
With them they took seven steeds,
There were no fairer under heaven
   That any man might see.
Into Germany they began to ride;
As a dealer of horses with much pride
   He seemed for to be.

The merchant was a true guide;
The earl and he began to ride together
   Until they came to that place.
A mile besides the castle
Where the Emperor began to live,

There was a rich abbey;
From the abbot, they got leave
To sojourn and make their horses fat;
    That was an noble occasion.
The abbot was the lady's uncle,
Because of her he was in great distress,
    And much mourning he made.

So it happened upon a day
To Church the earl took his way,
    In order to hear Mass.
He was a fair man and a tall [one;]
When the abbot saw him,
    He said, "Sir, come near.
Sir, when the Mass is done,
I pray you to eat with me at noon,
    If [it] be your wish."
The earl assented all with jest;
Before the meal, they washed all together,
    And to meat, they went together.

After meat, as I tell you,
Into the orchard they took their way,
    The abbot and the knight.
The abbot said and sighed sorely,
"Certainly, Sir, I live in care
    For a lady bright;
She is accused, my heart is troubled,
Therefore she shall go to [her] death
    All against the right;
Except she have help, indeed,
In a fire she shall be burnt
    This day next week."

The earl said, "So have I happiness,
Of her, methinks it is a great sorrow,
 If that she be true."
The abbot said, "By Saint Paul,
For her, I dare lay my soul
 That never guilty was she.
Such works she never wrought,
Neither in deed nor in thought,
 Save a ring so free
To the Earl of Toulouse she gave with pleasure
In ease from him and for no sin;
 In confession thus she told me."

The earl said, "Since it is so,
Christ avenge her of her woe,
 Who bought her with His blood.
Would you make me secure without fail,
For to hold true counsel;
 It might be for your good."
The abbot said by many books
And by his profession that he would conceal [it]
 And else he were mad.
"I am he that she gave the ring to
In order to be our token,
 Now conceal it for the cross.

"I am come, dear Sir,
To do battle for her,
 And thereto stand with right;
But first myself, I would shrive her,
And if I find her clean of life,
 Then will my heart be light,
Let me be put into monk's clothes

At that place men should lead her
　To be prepared for death;
When I have shriven her without fail
For her will I do battle,
　As I am a true knight."

The abbot was never so glad,
He grew nearly mad for joy,
　He began to kiss the earl;
They became merry and slew care
All that week he lived there,
　In mirth without loss.
That day the lady should be burnt
The earl with the abbot went
　In monk's clothing, indeed;
Before the Emperor he knelt quickly
So that he might shrive the lady;
　At once he is received.

He examined her surely,
As it says in the story;
　She was without guilt.
She said, "By Him that died on the tree,
Trespass, [there] was never any in me
　Wherefore should I be destroyed,
Save once without lying,
To the Earl of Toulouse, I gave a ring;
　Absolve me if you will.
But thus my destiny is come to an end,
So that in this fire I must be burnt;
　There God's will be done."

The earl absolved her with his hand,
And afterwards quickly he began to stand up,

And said, "Lordings, peace!
Ye that have accused this gentle lady,
Ye are worthy to be burnt."
    That one knight made a rush:
"You churl, monk, with all your skill,
Though your abbot be of her kin,
    Her sorrow thou shall not cease;
Rightly so would you say
Though all your convent had lain by her,
    So are ye evil and false."

The earl answered with free words,
"Sir, that one, I believe, you are
    [Who] has accused this lady.
Though we be men of religion,
Thou shall put to us without discourse
    For all the fare you made;
I [shall] prove for her thou sayst not right,
Lo, here [is] my glove to fight with thee,
    I understand this case;
As a false man I shall make thee known
In order to burn in a ready fire
    Thereto God give me grace."

All that stood in that place,
Thanked God for His grace,
    Without any fail.
The two knights were very angry;
He shall be dead, they swore great oaths,
    But it might not avail.
The earl went there besides [them,]
And armed himself with much pride,
    To assail his enemies.
Manfully, when they met together,

They hewed through helmet and basinet,
And ruined many a coat of mail.

They rode together without fault,
That one spear of his broke on him
   That other failed too.
The earl smote him with his spear,
Through the body he began to bear [on] him,
   To the ground he began to go.
So that the other saw and fast began to flee;
The earl overtook him under a tree,
   And wrought him much trouble;
There this traitor began to yield to him,
As a recreant in the field,
   He might not flee from him.

Before the Emperor they went,
And there he made him, truly,
   To speak for the occasion.
He said, "We thought to destroy her
Since she would not do our will,
   That is worthy in hopes."
The earl answered them then,
"Therefore, traitors, you shall burn
   In this fire both at once."
The earl at once seized them,
And in the fire he burnt them,
   Flesh, skin and bones.

When both these two were burnt,
The earl privately began to go
   To the rich abbey.
With joy and procession
They fetched the lady into the town,

With mirth, as I may tell.
The Emperor was very glad;
"Fetch me the monk," he commanded at once,
  "Why went he away so?
A bishopric, I will give him,
My help, my life, while I live,
  By God who owns this day."

The abbot knelt on his knee,
And said, "Lord, gone is he.
  To his own country;
He dwells with the Pope at Rome,
He will be very glad of his coming,
  I do [want] you to understand."
"Sir, abbot," said the Emperor,
"To me it was a dishonor,
  Such words I advise you to change;
At once in haste, that I [might] see him,
Or you shall never have good from me,
  And thereto, here [is] my hand."

"Lord," he said, "since it is so
That I must after him go,
  You must make me surety;
In case he has been your foe,
You shall not do him any harm;
  And then, also might I prosper,
After him I will go
So that you will be his friend,
  If [that] be your desire."
"Yes," said the Emperor very glad,
"Though he has slain all my kin,
  He is welcomed to me."

Then spoke the abbot in free words,
"Lord, I trust now in thee,
   You will do as you say;
It is Sir Barnard of Toulouse,
A noble and chivalrous knight,
   That has made the journey."
"Now, indeed," said the Emperor,
"It is a great dishonor to me;
   At once, Sir, I pray thee,
That you go after him,
We shall kiss and be good friends,
   By God who owns this day."

The abbot said, "I assent."
After the earl, at once he went,
   And said, "Sir, go with me.
My lord and yours, by Saint John,
Shall be made both at one,
   In order to be good friends."
Thereof the earl was very glad.
The Emperor came to him
   And said, "My friend so free
My wrath here I forgive thee;
My help, my love, while I live,
   By God who died on the tree."

Together lovely, they began to kiss;
Thereof all men had great happiness,
   The romances say so,
He made him steward of his land,
And put again into his hands
   What he had taken from him.
The Emperor lived but three years;
By election of the free lords

The earl they took then,
And made him their Emperor,
For he was valiant in battle
   To fight against his foe.

He wedded that lady to his wife;
With joy and mirth they led their life.
   Twenty years and three.
Between them they had children fifteen,
Doughty knights all also,
   And agreeable ones to see.
In Rome, this story is recorded,
A lay of Bretayne indeed called,
   And ever more shall be.
Jesus Christ bring us to Heaven,
There to have our home;
   Amen, Amen, for charity.

GUILD OF THE HOLY TRINITY
AND OF
SAINT WILLIAM OF NORWICH

In the name of the Father and Son and Holy Ghost, Three persons, one God in Trinity, and in honor of Our Lady, Saint Mary, His dear mother, and of Saint William, the holy, innocent and worthy martyr, and all saints: in the year of Our Lord Jesus Christ, one thousand, three hundred, seventy and six, the furriers and other good men began this guild and this brotherhood of Saint William, the holy innocent and martyr of Norwich; and all these ordinances underwritten, all the brothers and sisters shall hold and keep within their power.

At the first, all the brothers and sisters thus have promised that they, every year on the Sunday next after the feast of Saint Peter and Paul, in honor of the Trinity, and of Our Lady and St. William and all the saints, shall offer two ornamented candles before Saint William's tomb in the monastery of the Trinity, and every one of them offer a half penny at the Mass and hear all the Mass. And whosoever be absent, he shall then pay to Saint William's light, three pounds of wax; and it shall be raised and gathered by the alderman and his fellows. Also an innocent boy child shall carry a candle that day, the weight of two pounds, led between two good men, in token of the glorious martyr.

Also it is ordered that no man shall be excused by absence from that Mass, except it be for the King's service, or for dangerous sickness, or twenty miles dwelling from this city, so that he shall not pay the fine of three pounds of wax. And whosoever shall be excused for any other reason, it shall be at the alderman's wish and the company's.

Also all the brothers and sisters have ordained and assented to any ordinance that is made or shall be made amongst them, that they shall observe the King his right and no prejudice do against his law in these ordinances.

Also it is ordered that every brother and sister of this guild early on the morning of the guild day, shall hear a Mass of requiem for the souls of all the brothers and the souls of the sisters of this guild and for all Christian souls, at Saint William's altar in the monastery of the Trinity in Norwich and offer a farthing. And whosoever be missing, shall pay a pound of wax. And when the Mass is done, with the assent of the alderman, they shall all together go to and in, and every man that has property of the guild [shall] laid it down; and ordain there by their liking by common assent, and choose Officers for the next year. And who [shall] fail, shall pay three pounds of wax. And eighty men of the alderman's choosing, on the guild day, shall choose an alderman and two fellows and a summoner for the next year.

Also it is ordained, in honor of the Trinity, and of Our Lady, Saint Mary, and of Saint William and of all the saints, that what brother or sister, by God's sending, falls into trouble or disease and have nought to help himself, he shall have alms of every brother and sister every week, during his trouble, one farthing; from which farthings he shall have fourteen pence, and the remaining to go to the property. But if it is [because of] folly he shall not have of the alms.

Also it is ordered by common consent whosoever be chosen in office and refuses it, he shall pay, towards Saint

William's light, three pounds of wax and accordingly to the penalty of his oath.

Also if any brother or sister die, he shall have from the guild four torches, and four poor men clothed, about his corpse; and every brother and sister shall offer [prayers] at his Mass and await his entry and offer a farthing, and give a half penny for alms for the soul; and give a penny at the Mass, the which shall be gathered by the alderman and his fellows to do for the soul and all Christians. Also if any brother or sister die seven miles from the city, the alderman and another seven brothers at his funeral shall go in companionship to the corpse, and ordain and do for the soul as for one of the brethren.

Also it is ordered by common assent, that these brothers in honor of the Holy Trinity and Saint William shall eat together on that day at their common cost. And whosoever be summoned to do meeting or to congregate before the alderman and the brothers, and comes not, he shall pay a pound of wax to the light. Also it is ordered by common assent that no brother or sister shall be received into this guild except by the alderman and twelve brothers.

Also it is ordered by common assent that the common bellman shall go through the city on the guild day afternoon and call out the soul of the brothers and sisters of the guild by name and all Christian souls; and say that a Mass of requiem shall be said early in the morning, at the first hour of the day, in memory of the souls and of all Christians, and summon all the brothers and sisters that they be at the Mass at the altar of Saint William at the time of prime, upon the penalty of three pounds of wax.

JOHN MYRC'S INSTRUCTIONS FOR
PARISH PRIESTS

God sayeth Himself as we find written,
That where the blind leadeth the blind,
Into a ditch they both [shall] fall,
For they see not whereby they go.
So fares priests now by day;
They are blind to God's law,
That when they show advice to the people,
Into sin they do lead them.
Thus have they done now for many a year,
And all is for lack of learning;
Wherefore, you priest, curator,
If you [would] please thy Savior,
If you are not a great clerk,
Look you mostly to this work;
For here you might find and read
What [it] behooves thee to know by necessity,
How you shall preach to thy parish,
And what you need to teach them;
And what you must be thyself,
Here also you might see it.
For of little worth is thy preaching,
If you are of evil living.
    Priest, you thyself must be chaste,
And say thy service without haste,
That heart and mouth agree together,
If you desire that God hear you.
Of hand and mouth you must be true,
And great oaths you must eschew;

In word and deed you must be mild,
Both to man and to child.
Drunkenness and gluttony,
Pride and sloth and envy,
All [these] you must put away
If you desire to serve God to satisfaction.
Eat and drink what you need
But slay thy lusts in every thing.
Taverns also you must forsake,
And merchandise you shall not make;
Wrestling and shooting and such game
You must not use without blame;
Hawking, hunting, and dancing,
You must forego for any thing.
Slashed clothing and pointed shoes,
Thy good fame they would destroy.
Markets and fairs I forbid thee,
Except it be for thee more of a necessity.
In honest clothing, you must go,
A dagger or baldrick wear thee none;
Beard and crown you must have shaved,
If you wish to save thy order.
With meat and drink you must be free,
To poor and rich according to thy condition.
Earnestly you must read thy psalter,
And of Judgment Day have dread;
And ever do good against evil,
Or else thou might not live well.
Women's services you must forsake,
Lest they make thee of evil fame;
For women's speech that is from evil persons
Turns often away good virtue.
From foolish jokes and ribaldry
You must turn away your eyes;

Close thine eyes that you see not
The vanity of the cursed world.
Thus this world you must despise,
And holy virtues have in vision;
If you do thus, you shall be beloved
By all men who see and hear.

Thus also must you preach,
And thy parish earnestly teach;
When one has done a sin,
Look he lie not long therein,
But at once that he shrive himself,
Be it husband, be it wife,
Lest he forget by the days of Lent,
And out of mind it goes away.

Also you must satisfy thy God
Teaching thy parish thus and say.
All that are of maturity and age,
Who know to keep and rule themselves,
They shall all come to Church,
And be shriven all and some,
And be houseled without noise
On Easterday all together;
On that day by custom,
You shall be houseled all and some.
Teach them then with good intent,
To believe in the sacrament;
What they receive in form of bread,
It is God's body that suffered death
Upon the holy roodtree,
To atone for our sins and make us free.
Teach them then never later,
That in the chalice is but wine and water
That they receive in order to drink,
After that holy Eucharist.

Therefore you shall warn them
That they chew not that host too small,
Lest they do break it too small,
And in their teeth it does stick;
Therefore they should with water and wine
Cleanse their mouth that nothing is left therein:
But teach them all to believe fully,
That it that is made on the altar
It is truly God's blood
That He shed on the cross.
 Yet you must teach them more,
That when they do go to Church,
Then bid them leave their many words,
Their idle speech and foolish jests,
And put away all vanity,
And say their paternoster and ave.
None shall stand in Church,
Nor lean on the pillars nor the walls,
But fairly they should set themselves on [their] knees,
Kneeling down upon the floor,
And pray to God with a meek heart
To give them grace and mercy also.
Suffer them to make no noise,
But ever to be in their prayers;
And when the Gospel shall be read,
Teach them then to stand up all,
And cross themselves as fair as they can,
When the Gloria tibi is begun.
And when the Gospel is finished
Teach them often to kneel down soon;
And when they hear the bell ring
At that holy consecration,
Teach them to kneel down, both young and old,
And to hold up both their hands,

And say then in this manner,
Fair and soft without noise;
"Jesus, Lord, welcome be thou,
In the form of bread as I see thee;
Jesus for thy holy Name,
Shield me today from sin and shame;
Confession and Eucharist, Lord, grant me both
Before that I shall go hence,
And true contrition for my sins,
That I, Lord, never die therein.
And as thou were of a maiden born,
Suffer me never to be lost,
But when that I shall go hence,
Grant me the bliss without end. Amen."
Teach them thus, or some other thing,
To say at the Consecration.

Teach them also I pray thee,
That when they walk on the way
And see the priest coming towards them,
God's body with him carrying,
Then with great devotion,
Teach them there to kneel down.
Fair or foul, spare they nothing
To worship Him who wrought all.
For right glad may that man be
Who sees Him once in the day;
For so much good does that sight,—
As Saint Austin teaches aright,—
That day that you see God's body
These benefits shall you have securely:
Food and drink and all thy need,
Nor shall [anything] be wanting to thee that day.
Idle oaths and words also,
God forgives thee both;

Sudden death that same day
Dares thee not without any doubt.
Also that day I promise thee,
You shall not lose thine eyesight.
And every foot that you go then,
That holy sight in order to see,
They shall be told to stand in place
When you have need of them.

   Also within church and churchyard,
Do right as I tell you;
Song and cry and such fare,
You shall spare not anything in order to stop;
Casting the axletree and also of the stone,
Suffer them there to use none;
Balls and bars and such play,
Put away out of the churchyard.
Holding court and such manner of strife,
You must put out of the churchyard;
For Christ Himself teaches us
That holy church is His house,
That is made for nothing else
But to pray in as the book tells;
There the people shall gather within,
To pray and to weep for their sins.

   Teach them also well and prepare them,
How they shall pay their tithe.
Of all things that do renew them,
They shall tithe well and true;
After the custom of that country,
Every man shall pay his tithing,
Both of small and of great,
Of sheep and swine and other cattle.
Tithe of hire and of hand
Go with the custom of the land.

I hold it but an idle thing
To speak much of tithing,
For though a priest be but a fool,
He can ask well for his tithing.
  Witchcraft and sorcery,
You forbid them for any thing;
For whosoever believes in the fairy
Must believe thus in any way,
That it is a device of the devil
That makes a body to catch evil;
When he has prepared them with such believing,
That witchcraft shall save them,
So with charms and with fortune-telling,
He is brought again to health.
Thus by the fiend he is blinded,
And his belief is injured.

PROLOGUE
TO
THE CURSOR MUNDI

Men yearn in order to hear rimes,
And read romances in various forms:
Of Alexander the conqueror,
Of Julius Caesar the emperor,
Of the strange strife between Greece and Troy
Where many thousands lost their lives;
Of Brutus who was bold of hand,
The first conqueror of England;
Of King Arthur who was so powerful,
Of whom the like was not in his time;
Of wonders that happened to his knights
Of whose various adventures I hear tell,
As Gawain, Kay and other brave ones
In order to be of the round table;
How King Charles and Roland fought,
With the Saracens, they desired no agreement;
Of Tristrem and his dear Iseult,
How he for her became a fool;
Of Yonec and of Isambrace,
Of Idoine and of Amadace,
Stories as of several kinds of affairs
Of princes, prelates and of Kings,
Various songs of wonderful rime
In English, French and Latin;
Each one is ready to read and hear,
The things that they like best.
The wise man will hear in wisdom,

The fool draws himself near to folly;
The wrong is loath to hear of right,
And the proud become angry with humility;
Of chastity has the lecher hatred,
The angry ever make war on charity;
But by the fruit the wise may see
Of what strength is every tree.
Of all the kind of fruit that a man shall find
He fetches from the root of his kind;
From a good pear tree come good pears,
The worse the tree, the worse fruit it bears.
    That I speak of this very tree
Betokens man, both you and me.
This fruit betokens all our deeds,
Both good and ill which rightly is explained.
Our deeds from our heart take root,
Whether they be worthy of harm or help;
For by the things man draws to
Men shall know him for good or ill.
An example here for them I say
That rages in their riot ever;
In riot and boisterous conduct
Spend they the period of all their life,
For now none is held in regard
But who that can love a paramour.
That love folly, that [love] vanity,
They like now no other joy;
It is nothing but fancy for to say
Today it is, tomorrow away.
With chance of deed or change of heart,
What soft began has ending smart;
For when you think to be strongest,
From her will you [go,] and she from thee.
He that [you] think the strongest to stand

Beware of him, his fall is nearest at his hand;
Before he so violently is brought down
Whither to go he knows not,
His love has led him between
To such reward as he forthwith prayed for;
For then shall reward without hindrance
Be measured for deeds either better or worse.
     Therefore I bless that paramour
When I have need she gives me succor;
Who saves me first on earth from sin
And helps me to win Heavenly bliss.
For though I once have been untrue,
Her love is ever loyally new,
Her love she holds loyally,
That is sweeter than honey in the nest.
None such is found on earth,
For she is mother and maiden;
Mother and maiden never the less
Because from her Christ took his flesh
Who truly loves this mistress,
This is the love [that shall] never be gone
For in this love she never fails,
And in the other [life] she lasts forever.
From such a one you should take [the] matter [of poetry,]
Who can make skillful rimes,
To make both rime and song of her,
And love her sweet son among.
What help is [it] to set to labor
One thing that may not avail,
That is but fancy of this world
As you have seen and heard enough?
Matter find you large and broad,
Though many rimes of her be made;
Whosoever will tell of her fairness,

He shall find enough to tell.
Of her goodness and her truthfulness,
Men may find evermore to read;
Of sorrow, of love and charity,
There was never her equal nor shall ever be.
Lady is she of all ladies,
Mild and meek without bitterness,
For the oppressed the nearest to call on,
And raises the sinful when they fall.
In order to mend ever all our harm
Our Lord has made that sweet maid;
Thereby men may know her helping,
She prays ever for sinful men;
Who honor her, they may be bold;
She shall give them a hundredfold.

In her honor would I begin
A lasting work to think upon,
In order to make men know her kind
Who came to win such honor for us.
Some kinds of stories in order to show,
What was done in the old law,
Between the old law and the new
How Christ's birth began to geminate,
I shall show you with my purpose
Briefly from both testaments.
All this world, before this book ceases,
With Christ's help, I shall recount,
And tell some principal happenings,
For all, may no man have in a story.
But since no work may stand
Without a foundation to be lasting,
Therefore this work shall I establish
Upon a wonderful steadfast ground,

That is the Holy Trinity
That has made all with His beauty.
With Himself first I set my mark,
And afterwards to tell of His handiwork;
Of the angels that first fell,
And afterwards I will of Adam tell.
Of his offspring and of Noah,
And somewhat of his three sons;
Of Abraham and of Isaac
Who were holy without equal.
Afterwards I shall tell you
Of Jacob and Esau;
There shall next afterward be told
How that Joseph was bought and sold;
Of the Jews and Moses
Whom the people of God chose to lead them,
How God began to give him the law,
According to which the Jews should live;
Of Saul, the King, and of David,
How he fought against Goliath;
Afterwards of Solomon, the wise,
How wisely he did justice;
How Christ came according to the prophecies,
How He came to atone for his people.
And then you shall read it
Of Joachim and Saint Anne,
Of Mary also, her daughter mild,
How she was born and bore a child;
How He was born and when and where,
How she took him to the temple;
Of the Kings who sought Him,
Who brought to Him three presents;
How King Herod, with evil,

For the sake of Christ slew the children;
How the child fled to Egypt
And how He was led thence.
There shall you find some kinds of happenings
That Jesus did in His childhood;
Afterwards of John the Baptist
Who baptized Jesus in the river Jordan;
How Jesus when He had fasted long,
Was tempted by the wicked ghost;
Afterwards of John's baptizing,
And how King Herod beheaded him;
How Jesus Christ Himself
Chose for Himself twelve apostles,
And publicly began to preach
And to heal all who were sick,
And did miracles so frequently
That the Jews held him in strife;
Afterwards how the holy Lord
Turned water into wine,
Of five thousand men whom He
Fed with five loaves and three fishes.
Of a man afterwards you shall find
To whom He gave sight and [who] was born blind;
Of the adulterous woman
Whom the Jews deemed to stone;
How He healed one all disabled
Who was sick thirty and eight years;
How Magdalen with weeping
Came in order to wash Our Lord's feet,
Of her and Martha who was eager
About the needs of their house;
Of the dead Lazarus, laid under the loam,
How Jesus raised his body;
How the Jews after surrounding Jesus

And because of His sermon, threatened [Him] tyran-
    nically;
How they shed His blessed blood
And put Him upon the cross.
By Christ's will then I shall tell
How afterwards He plundered Hell;
How the Jews with their great evil purpose
Thought to render useless His resurrection;
How He arose, how He ascended,
Many men stood by and saw;
How He who is the most of the mighty
Sent to earth His Holy Ghost;
Some kinds of happenings of the twelve apostles,
But how they ended at the last.
How Our Lady ended and yielded
Her happy soul, it shall be told:
Of the holy cross, how it was made known
Long after that it was concealed;
Of the anti-Christ's coming, that shall be bold.
And of the fifteen dreary days
That shall come before doomsday.
Afterwards of the judgment, I shall tell you
Then of Our Lady's mourning courage
For she saw her son on the rood.
The last discourse of all this colloquy
Shall be of her conception.

These are the matters explained in a row
That I think to draw in this book
Shortly riming on the deed
For many are they to prosper hereof.
Useful me thinks it is for man
To know himself how he began;
How he began to breed in this world,
How his offsprings began to spread;

Both of the first and of the last
Through what kind of course, this world is passed.
After Holy Church's state
This same book, it is translated,
Into the English tongue to read
For the love of the English people,
The English people of England,
For the common to understand.
    French rimes I heard read
Commonly in every place;
It is made mostly for Frenchmen,
What is [it] to him [who] knows no French?
The people of England,
Are Englishmen there altogether;
The speech that men may prosper with most,
To speak most therewith is of necessity.
Seldom, for any reason, was
The English tongue praised in France;
We give each one their language,
I think we do them no outrage.
For the unlearned Englishman, I narrate
Who understands what I tell,
And to them I speak most of all
Who are wont to waste in idleness
Their lives in trifles and begging,
To be aware of that very thing and be guided
Somewhat to attend to that thing,
That all these might amend [their lives] with courage.
Very bad have they spent that spending,
That find no fruit thereof at the end.
Skillful words and work as we are inclined to,
Confidently we shall pay the accounting;
Therefore do draw them hitherward
That will have part of the pardon;

Shall have pardon to hear and hold
Of [their] plight with Christ's blessing.
Now of this prologue will we cease,
In Christ's name our book begins;
Courser of the world, men ought to call it,
For it recounts almost all.
Take we our beginning then
Of Him who began all this world.

THE DEATH OF SAINT ANDREW

Saint Andrew, Christ's dear apostle,
While he went in this world here,
Very many people in several countries
He converted to the Christian truths;
And at the last, as it happened,
[He went] into a city where he began to dwell.
    A judge was in that city,
And his name was called Egeas;
A man who lived in idolatry
And in false gods, full of envy.
He gathered together both bond and free,
Rich and poor of every country,
And ordered that they should make sacrifice
Unto his gods of much high esteem;
And whosoever would not make offerings,
Great vengeance would he take on them.
    The people very quickly then sought thither
And made worship to the devil.
And soon when Saint Andrew heard tell
Of that foul behavior how it happened,
Thither he began to pass very certainly,
And thus said to Egeas:
"Since you covet that people know you
As a judge over all other men,
Then you should know in deed and constitution
Thy judge, that is God in Heaven,
Who shall judge thee after death.
It is necessary for to know Him now;
He is thy God and mighty over all,

And all others are false idolatry;
Him you ought to honor for evermore,
And truly know Him for thy God,
And draw thy heart away from devils,
That lead to pain that lasts forever."
   Egeas then answered back:
"Thy words," he said, "are all in vain,
And you tell nothing of truth to me
That I may prove by proper skill;
For, while your God, whom you call on
Preached to the people everywhere on the earth,
And taught His men who lived with Him
To preach the same that you tell here,
By the Jews here was He taken
And nailed to and hanged high on the tree;
And had He been God as you say,
It had not been so, by any means.
Therefore I say thy words are vain."
   Saint Andrew then answered again:
"And could you clearly know and see
The strength of that very holy tree
That is called the cross in the land,
Then would you know and understand
How Jesus Christ, my Master free,
By reasonable cause of charity,
And for pity that He had in mind
Of the great troubles of mankind,
He put Himself to pain of the cross,
Not in spite of Himself but by His will."
   Egeas then unto this thing
Answered as in great scorn;
He said, "How may you say these sayings,
Since that you know the truth well yourself?

At the first time He was betrayed,
And through one of His own retainers,
And afterwards taken boldly by the Jews,
And bound and led forth between them
To the quickest gate of Caiaphas' hall,
And from there to Sir Pilate;
There was He judged to hang on the cross,
As the Jews ordered among themselves.
In spite of Him, they began to destroy him,—
How prove you then it was His will?"

Saint Andrew said, "His will it was
That may I prove well before I pass;
Of His retainers myself was one
At the same time when He was taken,
And before the time He was betrayed
To us all together thus He said,
How He should be sold for men's sins,
And suffer full many a pain
And die on the cross exactly as you tell,
For the health of men's souls and for nothing else,
And on the third day full rightly arise.
These words He told us in this manner;
Therefore I tell you in this place,
That with His will He suffered death."

Egeas then thought in great scorn,
And to Saint Andrew said he quickly:
"You have learned in a simple school,
Thy preaching proves thyself a fool;
For whether it was His will or not,
You grant that He was put on the cross,
And He was hanged as I said before;
And therefore leave that lazy person's teaching
And make offerings unto my gods,

Or else I shall for the sake of thy God
Make thee hang right on such a tree
As you say [you] should be so honored.
For fouler death may no man have
Therefore on thee I grant it."

    Saint Andrew then without anger
Said, "Indeed, that is my greatest desire.
I wish to be worthy for His sake
Upon a cross my death to take;
Thereto shall I ever be ready
For any pain that you may do to me."

    Egeas then with great envy,
Sent after all his instruments of torture,
And bade them briskly among themselves
To order a cross for him to hang on,
And fastened thereto both hands and feet
So that none of them met with the other.
"Fasten him with no nails I advise,
To make him hastily to be dead so,
But bind him to [the cross] with strong ropes
So that he may be pained long."

    To do his bidding were they prompt;
A cross they made with all their might,
And hands on him then fast they fastened,
To do him pain they were very pressed.
They led him through that city
To the place where he should be hanged.
And all the people that lived thereabouts
Gathered together in a very great crowd.
And all thus they said among themselves:
"Alas, this working is all wrong;
What has this righteous man done ill
That you in this way will destroy him?

This noble man who never did privation,
Very innocent suffers he all this;
Very innocent be he put on the rood,
And innocent shall men spill his blood,
For he has ever been happy and glad
To mend all men that had need."
   Saint Andrew then prayed for the people
And thus he said to all of them:
"Go back, I pray you all
And hinder me not this day of joy;
Distrub not now my passion,
For unto bliss it makes me bound."
And soon when Saint Andrew beheld
The cross before him in the field,
Unto God made he his prayer,
And to the cross in this manner
He cried and said with a very great voice:
"Hail be thou, holy and blessed cross,
That is hallowed and glorified
With Christ's members on every side;
And honored art thou with His bones,
Well better than with precious stones.
With joyful heart I come to thee,
So that you gladly receive me,
Disciple of Him without equal
Who hanged on thee, my Master dear.
Now are you ready to hang me on,
That I in heart have desired long;
I have loved thee with heart and will.
And desired ever to come to thee."
Before the cross then he knelt down
And thus he made his prayer:
"Ah, noble cross of great bounty,
From earthly men receive me now,

And yield me to my good Master
So that He with mild mind may
Receive me from thee whom He made,
As He through thee brought me from harm;
No better bed I have to buy."
Then he put off his outer garments;
To the persecutors he began to pray for them
And bade [that] they should do forth their deed.
   The persecutors when this was said,
Took his body with bitter stratagem
Onto the cross they began to tie it,
And fastened very firmly both hands and feet;
And all his body very fast they bound
As Egeas had commanded them.
When he was so bound, stretched out
They let him hang and they went home.
People gathered very fast about him
Of all that country in great crowd;
He held his eyes up to Heaven,
And thus he said with joyous voice:
"I see my Lord, God Almighty,
And in His sight now here I stand."
Upon the cross there alive he hung
Two days, preaching among the people;
That was very long such pain to feel,
But with Christ he was well comforted.
Twenty thousand people were there
To hear him preach, with sorrowful hearts.
When the first day was come to an end,
All those people by one assent
To Egeas' house they ran fast,
And said they should burn him all alive,
Except he quickly prepare to take him down
Who was hanged against reason.

"He is a righteous man," they said,
"And has done well both night and day;
A good teacher has he ever been,
And more truthful was never seen,
And such a man, Sir, for certain
Should not suffer so hard pains;
Therefore except he be taken down soon,
In evil times was that deed done."

Egeas dreaded the anger of the people,
And down he promised to take him;
And forth he went with them in haste,
Both he and all his instruments of torture.
The people thronged about all in a body;
And when Saint Andrew saw them coming,
Because of their coming he was not satisfied,
And to Egeas thus he said:
"Whereto come you unto me,
Except you desire to believe in Jesus free,
And leave thy idols more or less
And pray to Jesus for forgiveness?
If you will not in this manner do,
Run fast before vengeance comes to thee,
You get no force nor power
To approach my body nor take it down;
My Lord will lend me that favor
That alive I shall not be taken down."

Then the tormentors, with eager mood,
Went to him, as they were mad.
They pulled at him with very great force,
But nothing of him might they stir;
Their arms and hands soon in haste
They grew dry as they were refuse flax;
As they cast up their arms to him
As dry sticks then stood they still.

Saint Andrew then made his prayers
To Almighty God in this way.
He said, "Lord, if it be Thy will,
In this place let me hang still,
That no one have power to take me down
Down from this cross that I dwell on,
Until that time Thyself grants
For me to have the bliss of Heaven;
But let me hang still as I do
Until the time You take my soul to You."
When this was said, there came a light
Down from Heaven with bright beams,
And covered his body about.
The people therefore had much fear;
They might not look because of the great light
At his body, so bright was it.
And as the light was most of all
To God in Heaven, he gave his ghost.

   Egeas was very fearful then,
And in terror he ran home fast;
But, on the way, before he came home,
He suffered death with much shame.
So sudden sorrow was sent to him,
As was worthy, he went to woe.
Saint Andrew's soul, with angels' voices
And in that light was lifted to Heaven
Where he arrived into everlasting bliss;
Almighty God thither [take] us also.

   Egeas had a worthy wife
Who loved Saint Andrew in his life;
For him, she ordered a monument,
And buried his body with true intent.
And from his grave, as men might see,
Sprang up oil, full fair plenty

That was medicine to more or less
That thither sought for several illnesses.
And by that oil, as the book says,
All that country took example;
For when it sprang on several sides
Then they hoped to have a good year
Of corn and fruit and other things;
And when they saw it scarcely spring
Then they hoped to have scant of corn
And of fruit as I said before.

TREATISES OF RICHARD ROLLE OF HAMPOLE

I On the Nature of the Bee

The bee has three characteristics. One is that she is never idle and she is not with them that will not work, but casts them out and puts them away. Another is that, when she flies, she takes earth on her feet so that she be not raised too high in the air of the wind. The third is that she keeps her wings bright and clean. Thus, righteous men that love God are never in idleness: for either they are in work, praying or thinking or reading or other good doing, or reproving idle men and showing them worthy to be put from the rest of Heaven for they will not work here. They take earth, that is, they hold themselves vile and earthly so that they be not blown with the wind of vanity and of pride. They keep their wings clean; That is, the two commandments of charity, they fulfil in good conscience and they have other virtues unblemished with the filth of sin and unclean lust. Aristotle says that the bees are fighting against him who will draw their honey from them; so should we do against the devils that force them to rob from us the honey of a poor life and grace. For many there are who can never hold their friends, related or strangers, in the order of gentle love, but either they love them too much, or they love them too little, setting their thoughts unrighteously on them, or they love too little if they do not all as they desire for them. Such can not fight for their honey, because the devils turn it to worms and make their souls oftimes very bitter in angers and vexations and care of vain thoughts and other wretchedness; for they are so heavy

in earthly friendship that they might not flee into the love
of Jesus Christ, in which they might well forego the love
of all creatures living on earth. Wherefore, accordingly,
Aristotle says that some birds are of good flight that can
pass from one land to another. Some are of ill flight for
heaviness of body and because their nests are not far from
the earth. Thus it is for them who turn themselves to God's
service. Some are of good flight because they fly from earth
to Heaven and rest them there in thought and are fed in
the delight of God's love and have no thought of love of
the world. Some [there] are who can not fly from this
land, but on the way let their hearts rest and delight themselves in various loves of men and women, as they come and
go, now one and now another. And in Jesus Christ they
can find no sweetness; or if they, at any time, feel [they]
ought, it is so little and so short because of other thoughts
that are in them, that it brings them to no stability. Or
they are like to a fowl that is called ostrich or stork that has
wings and it may not fly because of the weight of the body.
So they have understanding and fast and watch and seem
holy to men's sight, but they might not fly to love and con-
templation of God, they are so weighed down with other
affections and other vanities.

II   A Notable Treatise from the Ten Commandments
Drawn by Richard, the hermit of Hampole

The first commandment is, "Thy Lord God you shall
worship and to Him only you shall serve." In this commandment is forbidden all idolatries, all witchcraft and
charmings, the which may do no remedy to any sickness of
man, woman, or beast, for they are the snares of the devil by
the which he attempts himself to deceive mankind. Also in
this commandment is forbidden to give truth to sorcery or to
divining by the stars or by dreams or by any such things.

Astrologers behold the day, the hour, and the place that man is born in and under which sign he is born and the point that he begin to be in and by their signs and others, they say that that shall happen to the man afterwards; but their errors are reproved by the holy doctors. Men shall worship holy crosses for they are the sign of Christ crucified. To images is the loving that is to them of whom they are the images; for that intention only they are for to worship. The second commandment is, "Thou shall not take the name of God in vain." Here is forbidden oaths without motive. He who names God and swears falsely, despises God. In three ways, many may sin in swearing; that is, if he swears against his conscience, or if he swears by Christ's wounds or blood, that is evermore great sin, though it be true, for it sounds in irreverence of Jesus Christ. Also if he comes against his oath, not fulfilling what he has sworn. The name of God is taken in many ways—with heart, with mouth, and with works. With heart, false Christian men take it in vain, who receive the sacrament without grace in the soul. With the mouth, it is taken in vain, with all oath breaking; of new preaching that is vanity and lack of devotion; prayers when we honor God with our lips and our heart is far from Him. With works, hypocrites take God's name in vain, for they fain good deeds without and they are without charity and virtue and strength of soul to stand against all ill stirring. The third commandment is, "Remember thee that thou be holy on the holyday." This commandment may be taken in three ways: first, generally, that we cease from all vices; second, specially, that we stop all bodily works that stop devotions to God in praying and thinking; the third is special, as in contemplative men that separate themselves from all worldly things so that they give themselves holy to God. The first way is needful for us to do, the second we ought to do, the third is perfection;

because on the holyday men ought, as God bids, to leave all sin and do no work that stops them to give their hearts to God so that they be holy that day in rest and devotion and deeds of charity.

The fourth commandment is, "Honor thy father and thy mother." That is in two things, that is, in body and in spirit; in body, in sustenance that they be helped and sustained in their old age and when they are feeble of themselves; in spirit, in reverence and obedience that they say to them no word of evil speaking, nor dishonesty, nor of displeasure unadvisedly but serve them meekly and gladly and loyally that they may win what God promised to such children, that is, land of light. And if they be dead, they ought to help their souls with almsgivings and prayers. The fifth commandment is, that, "Thou slay no man, neither with assent nor with word or favor." And also here is forbidden the unrighteous harming of any person. They are slayers in spirit who will not feed the poor in need and who defame men and who confound the innocents. The sixth commandment is, "Thou shall be no unchaste person." That is, you shall have no man nor woman except whom thou has taken according to the ritual of Holy Church. Also here is forbidden all manner of willful pollution, procured in any manner against kindly use or other ways.

The seventh commandment is, "Thou shall not do any theft." In the which is forbidden all manner of withdrawing of other men's things wrongly against their will who own it, except it be in time of most need when all things are common. Also here is forbidden deceit of weight, or of story, or of food, or of measure, or through usury or violence or fear, as beadles and foresters do and ministers of the King, or through extortion as lords do. The eighth commandment is that, "Thou shall not bear false witness against thy neighbor," as in assize or cause of matrimony. And also lying is forbidden in this commandment and forswearing. But all lyings are not deadly sin except they be troublesome to some man in body or in spirit. The ninth commandment is, "Thou shall not covert the house, or other thing, mobile or immobile, of thy neighbor wrongly." Nor shall thou hold other men's goods if you may give them back, else thy penance saves thee not. The tenth commandment is, "Thou shall not covert thy neighbor's wife, nor his servants, nor his maidens, nor the movables of his." He loves God who keeps these commandments for love. His neighbor he ought to love as himself that is, to the same good that he loves himself to, no thing to ill; and that he love his neighbor's soul more than his body or any part of the world.

A METRICAL HOMILY
THE SIGNS OF THE DOOM

Today Saint Luke tells us,
In our Gospel that Jesus
Spoke of the thing that is to come,
And namely of the Day of Doom.
Signs he said shall be done
Both in the sun and in the moon,
And in the stars all together;
And people shall suffer misery and vexation;
For people shall perish for the din of the sea
And for trouble that then shall be.
Over all the world [shall] be redness,
Misery and ugliness,
For the mighty powers of the heavens
Shall be startled by that voice;
Then shall Christ come that men might see
In majesty and in great power.
When this begin for to be,
Look up and ye may see
That your salvation and your reward
Have very nearly come to you.
Himself our salvation, He is called,
For He bought us when He was sold.
    When Christ had said this horrible saying,
An example He began to show
And said, "When ye see the leaves of spring,
And the trees bring forth fruit,
Then know ye well that summer is nigh";
Also may you know in this manner,

When you see these signs in the land,
That Christ is very nearly come.
"For heaven and earth shall pass away
But my word passes never more";—
Yet who sees the thing that I tell you
Neither may nor might ruin nor destroy.—
"When this world that I made from nothing
Shall be gone and brought to an end,
Then shall My word be true,
For My kingdom shall last ever."
This is the strength of our Gospel
As man with English tongue may tell.

   The master in the Gospel preaches
And says that Christ teaches us therein
In order to forsake this world's pleasures,
Full of wretchedness and sin;
For Christ told us how it shall end,
And warns us very well as a friend.
He tells us of the active signs,
Where He begins His Gospel,
And says, "Kingdom shall savagely rise
Against kingdom and make men horrified,
For calamity shall make the heroes bleed,
And make in the land hunger and need;
This calamity shall brew trouble quickly,
And destroy much of this world's joy."
Such words said Christ of these wars
That harm people in the world very severely;
For what kind of war shall fall on the land
To poor people it is shown most grievously.
That Holy Church now feels well
To whom trouble has been very distasteful;
For it [the church] and the poor men both have
Rich and poor of their injury

This trouble tortures the pride of the poor,
As they well know who walk widely,
But have worlds and high towers
To guard their city and men from battles;
Therefore rich men have ever indeed
Enough of food and drink and happiness,
But the poor suffer the trouble
Who have lack of clothing and food.
And therefore Jesus warns both,
Rich and poor of the injury
Where He shows in the Gospel
Signs that behooves us to cut down our pride.
  He said [these] signs shall be done
Both in the sun and in the moon;
The sun shall turn into darkness,
As says Joel who bears witness
Of Christ who shows us these signs
In our Gospel with horrible words.
For the moon shall be turned
Into blood that people shall see;
When sun and moon shall turn in this way,
Then shall the sinful sorely hasten,
For then may they know clearly
That Christ shall come to them in haste.
But good men shall dread nothing,
For then shall they be sure of reward,
In that blissful land that they
Shall ever live in sport and play.
And Christ in our Gospel therefore
Comforts us very mildly
And bids us look to the growing trees;
For when men see leaves on them,
Men know that very near is summer coming,
And rightly as we may understand,

When we see these signs come,
That near at hand is the Day of Doom.
   But for Christ speaks of signs,
That shall bring tidings of Doom,
Therefore [it] is good that I tell you
Some of these active signs.
Saint Jerome tells that fifteen
Fearful signs shall be seen
Before the Day of Doom and shall
Each one fall on various days.
The first day shall all the sea
Swell and rise and be higher
Than any mountain of all the land,
And as a mountain up it shall stand;
The height thereof shall pass the mountains
By sixty feet as Jerome tells;
And as much the second day,
Shall it settle and wilt away,
And be lower than it is now.
For water shall it have much less.
The third day, porpoises and whales,
And other great fishes all,
Shall yell and make so sorrowful noise
That sorrowful it shall be to hear.
The fourth day freezes the water, and the sea
Shall burn as fire and glowing be.
The fifth day shall grass and trees
Sweat bloody dew that [shall] be horrible.
The sixth day shall fall down
The works of the world, both towers and halls.
The seventh day shall great stones
Smit together and beat fiercely.
And all the earth, the eighth day,
Shall shake and quake and strike all the people.

The ninth day, all the mountains
[Shall] be made all even with the earth.
The tenth day shall people creep up,
As mad men from deep pits.
The eleventh day, shall bones arise
And stand on the graves where men now lie.
The twelfth day, shall the stars fall.
The thirteenth day, shall all men die
To rise with the other dead men
And come with them to the great court.
The fourteenth day, suddenly
Shall both burn, both earth and air.
The fifteenth day, they both
Shall be made new and fair very quickly;
And all dead men shall arise
And shall come before Christ, Our justice.
  Then shall Christ judge as King very wise,
And make the sinful sorely horrified;
So horrible shall He be to them,
That they were lief that they might flee
From that judgment that He shall judge,
Then all this world; so be He excellent
To them that sinfully come there;
And therefore shall they weep bitterly
And say, "Alas, that we were born,
Shamefully have we lost ourselves."
Then shall all their wicked deeds
Stand and call against them
And with their sign bear witness
Of their sins and their wickedness.
Of many sorrows shall they tell,
For Satan with many companions,
To bind them he shall be very quick
And fiercely draw them into Hell;

Where they shall evermore dwell
And woefully well up in pains
And continually tell of sorrow.
   This is their doom that here in sin
Lie and their sins will not cease;
But would they think about Judgment Day,
It behooves them to leave their plightful play.
Alas, alas, what shall they say
Before Him that mighty kinsman,
When all the men that was and is
Shall see their sins more or less,
And all the angels of Heaven,
And more fiends than men may name?
Contradiction may there not be
Of things that all men may see.
Of this openly showing
God has showed many signs;
Of a sign I have heard tell,
That happens well in our Gospel.
   A black monk of an abbey
Was a superintendent, as I heard say;
He was held [to be] a holy man
Among his fellows every one.
A cloistered monk loved him very well,
And was to him very special,
For frequently together drawn
Faithful friends and good fellows.
It happened that this superintendent of infirmary
Was sick and he who was dear to him
Came to make him happy and glad
And to make known his friendship to him;
He asked him how he felt himself,
And he told to him all his condition,
And said, "Very cruelly I feel myself,

I draw [near] to death as you may see."
　His fellow was sorry for him
And prayed to him very earnestly therefore,
That if God did his will to him
That he should show his state to him.
This sick monk promised to come to him
If he might get leave thereof;
"I shall," he said, "if I may
Come to thee, my state to tell."
　When this was said, he died soon [after,]
And his fellow asked his favor
And prayed to God for His mercy,
That He should show him openly,
Either waking or sleeping,
Some news of his fellow;
And as he lay upon a night,
His brother came with the brightness of light
And told him both of Heaven and of Hell.
And he prayed he should tell him
His state; and he said, "I fare well,
Through the help of Our Lady;
She was not aware I had begun
To dwell in Hell with Satan."
His fellow thought fairly thereof
And asked him wherefore and why
And said, "We all thought well that you
Have been a holy man until now;
How shall it fare with us wretches
That in sin and folly live
When you that led so holy a life
Was judged to Hell to follow?
　When this was said, the dead answered
And told his fellow how he acted;
And said, "Soon when I gave [up] the ghost,

To my doom was I led in haste,
And as I stood to hear my doom
Before Jesus with a dreary face,
From the fiends I heard many upbraidings,
And a book was laid before me
That was the rule of St. Benedict,
That I promised to hold and yet [hold.]
This rule they made me read rapidly
And as I read, I began to dread sorely,
For omissions might I make none,
But of the clauses every one
I yielded an account, how I held them,
And my conscience began to accuse me.
It showed there very openly
That I led my life wrongly;
For in the rule is many a passage
That was then brought against me
Wherethrough I had almost there
Been judged for to go to Hell.
Except I loved our Lady well
While I lived, therefore I had
Very good help through her mercy.
For she besought Christ inwardly
That I might in Purgatory
Cleanse my sins and my folly.
Therefore I hope to go very well,
For my sorrow shall soon cool;
Therefore, my friend, I pray thee,
That you make the fellows pray for me."
When this was said, he went away,
And his fellow moaned very much for him,
And after this sight, many a day,
He prepared to pray for his soul.
  This tale have I told you

To show in what manner and how
We shall be judged and yield an account
What our sins may amount to;
For all shall come to gnashing with teeth, certainly,
Where that they are mistaken
By the least idle thought,
For there forgiveness is not of right.
Then shall we atone dearly for the sins
For which we are not shriven here;
If we here be shriven of sin,
Where God has forgiven us of them,
Therefore [it] behooves us to beat our sins here
With shrift of mouth and wet cheeks.
For shrift of mouth is medicine
That shields man from Hell's pains,
For if we confess ourselves clean of sin
With penance, in death we shall have joy,
And may be sure on Doomsday
To go to the blissful place
Where Christ shall ever more be King;
For His mercy, He brings us thither. Amen.

THE SONGS OF LAWRENCE MINOT

I

Listen and I shall tell to you
The Battle of Halidon Hill

True King who sits on the throne
   Unto Thee I tell my tale,
And from Thee I bid a boon,
   For You are remedy of all my harm.
As You made the earth and the moon,
   And beasts and fowls, great and small,
Unto me send Thy help soon
   And make straight my deeds in this dale.

In this dale, I droop and lie concealed,
   For secret deeds that did me harm,
For England, had my heart great care
   When Edward proceeded first to war.
The Frenchmen were bold to go
   Against him with shield and spear;
They turned again with sad sides,
   And all their pomp not worth a pear.

A pear of value is more sometimes
   Than all the boast of Normandy.
They sent their ships on every side
   With flesh and wine and wheat and rye;
With heart and hand, it is not to be hidden,
   For they began to hasten to help Scotland;

They fled and dared no deed abide,
   And all their fare not worth a fly.

For all their fare they dared not fight,
   For dint of death had they such fear;
Of Scotland had they never sight
   Ever while they were of stout words.
They would have behaved themselves at their might
   And busy were they there about;
Now God help Edward in his right,—
   Amen—and all his ready army.

His ready army might Jesus speed.
   And save them both by night and by day;
That the Lord of Heaven might lead Edward,
   And aid him as He might well.
The Scots now all wide will spread;
   For they have failed at their prayers;
Now are they lurking all for dread,
   Who were before so stout and gay.

Gay were they and well they thought
   Of the Earl of Moray and others more;
They said it should be bought very dearly
   The land that they were fleeing from.
Philip Valois made words,
   And said he should slay their enemies;
But all the words were for nought,
   They think to be met, if they were more.

More threats yet have they made,
   Ill-will might they have for reward;
And many nights as they have waked
   To destroy all England with their deeds.

But, love of God, the pride is loosened
  From them that were so bold on steed;
And some of them are left all naked
  Not far from Berwick on the Tweed.

A little from that forementioned town,
  Halidon Hill that is the name,
There was cracked many a crown
  Of wild Scots and also of tame.
There was their banner borne all down,
  To make such boast they were to blame;
But nevertheless ever were they bound
  To injure England with sorrow and shame.

Shame they have as I hear say;
  At the Dundee now is done their dance,
And they go mostly another way
  Even through Flanders into France.
To Philip Valois fast they cry
  There for to dwell and him advance;
And nothing pleased them [more] than to play
  After this sorry chance is happened to them.

This sorry chance is happened to them,
  For they were false and wonderously cruel;
For cursed caitiffs were they shown [to be]
  And full of treason, truth to tell.
Sir John Comyn had they hid,
  They did kill him in Holy Church;
And therefore many a Scotch bride
  With grief was prepared where they must dwell.

There dwelt the King, the truth to say,
  With his household a little while;

He gave good comfort in that country
　　To all his men about a mile.
Although his men were great of might,
　　Ever they doubted them of treachery;
The Scots' tricks might gain nothing,
　　For they all stumbled at that stile.

Thus in that battle they left their lives
　　Who were before so proud in praise;
Jesus, by Thy five wounds,
　　Help us to have peace in England.

II

*Now for to tell you, will I turn
to the Battle of Bannockburn*

Scots out of Berwick and of Aberdeen,
At the Bannock brook were you to clean;
There you slew many innocent ones, as it is seen,
And now has King Edward avenged it, I know.
　　It is avenged, I know, well worth the while;
　　It was with the Scots and they were full of deceit.

Where were you, Scots of Saint John's town?
The boast of your banner is beaten all down;
When you will offer boasting, Sir Edward is bound
For to increase your care and crack your crown.
　　Few remedy his harms, well worth the while,
　　Shame betide the Scots for they are full of deceit.

Scots of Sterling were stern and bold,
Of God or of good men had they no fear;
Now have they, the robbers, pricked about,
But at the last Sir Edward plundered their army;

He has plundered their army, well worth the while,
But ever are they under both trick and deceit.

Rough-foot rivelings, now increase thy care
Bag-bearers with thy boasting, thy dwelling is bare;
False wretch and forsworn, whither will you go?
Go thou into Bruges and abide there;
    There, wretch, shall thou live and weary the while,
    Thy dwelling in Dundee is done for thy guile.

The Scots go to Bruges and beat the streets,
All these Englishmen's harms, they threaten;
Fast makes he his moan to the men that he meets,
But few friends he finds that his calamity remedy:
    Few remedy his harms, well worth the while,
    He uses all menaces with trick and deceit.

But many men threaten and speak full of ill
That sometimes was better to be stone-still;
The Scot in his words has wind for to destroy,
For at the last, Edward shall have all his will:
    He had his will at Berwick, well worth the while;
    Scots brought him the keys, but [he] took care of
        their guile.

III

*How Edward the King came to Brabrant
and took homage of all the land*

God who created both sea and sand,
Save Edward, King of England,
Both body, soul and life,
And grant him joy without strife;
For many men are angry with him

In France and Flanders too;
For he defends fast his right,
And thereto Jesus grant him might,
And so to act both night and day,
That it may be to God's satisfaction.
    Our King was come, truth to tell,
Into Brabrant in order to dwell.
The Emperor Louis of Bavaria,
That in that land then had no equal,—
He and also his two sons
And other princes many more;—
Bishops and prelates were many there
Who had very much worldly wealth,
Princes and people, old and young,
All who spoke with the Dutch tongue,—
They all came with great honor
To save and help Sir Edward,
And proffered him, with all their advice,
In order to hold the King's place.
The Duke of Brabrant first of all
Swore, for things that might happen,
That he should, both day and night,
Help Sir Edward in his right,
In town, in field, in park and fen;
This swore the Duke and all his men,
And all the lords who arrived with him,
And thereto they held up their hands.
Then King Edward took his rest
At Antwerp which he liked best;
And there he made his money plain
That no man should talk there again;
His money that was good and loyal
[He] left in Brabrant, a very great amount;
And all that land until today

Fares the better for that journey.

When Philip Valois heard of this,
Thereat he was very angry, certainly;
He made his barons assemble,
Princes and lords of many towns.
At Paris they took their counsel,
Which points might avail them most;
And in every way they bethought themselves
To destroy England and bring [it] to nought.

Shipmen were soon sent after
To hear the King's commandment,
And the galley men also
Who knew both the weal and woe.
He commanded them that men should go
To England and nothing to spare,
But to burn and slay both man and wife
And child that none should remain alive;
The galley men held up their hands
And thanked God for their messages.

At Hampton, as I understand,
Came the galleys into the land,
And very fast they burnt and slew,
But not so much as some men think;
For, before they were gone they met
With men who soon stopped their sport.
Some were knocked on the head
So that the body remained there;
Some lay staring at the stars,
And some lay with their brains knocked out;
Then with them was no other joy,
But they who might flee were very glad.
The galley men, the truth to say,
Must of necessity turn another way;
They sought the streams far and wide

In Flanders and in Seland side.
   Then saw they where Christopher stood
At Yarmouth, upon the flood;
Then they went thither all together,
The galley men with bold hearts,
Eight and forty galleys and more,
And with them also went two transports,
And many other of small galleys,
With a great number of small boats;
They all tarried on the flood
To steal Sir Edward's good men.
Edward, our King, then was not there,
But soon when it came to his ear
He assembled his men full still,
And said to them what was his will.
Each man made himself ready then;
Then went the King and all his men
Onto their boats very quickly,
Also men who were doughty in deed.
They found the galley men in great number,
A hundred ever against one;
The Englishmen pushed them into war
Very boldly with bow and spear;
They slew there of the galley men
Ever sixty against ten,
So that some lie yet in that mire,
All headless without recompense.
The Englishmen were well armed
Both in iron and in steel;
They fought very fast both day and night,
As long as [their] might lasted them;
But the galley men were so many
That the Englishmen grew extremely weary;
They sought help but none came there,

Then unto God they made their moan.
But since the time that God was born,
Nor a hundred years before,
Were men never better in fight
Than the Englishmen while they had might.
But soon they began to miss all mastery;
God bring their souls to His bliss,
    Listen now, and believe me,
Whoso live, they shall see
That [they] remember it was dearly bought
What their galley men have wrought.
They tarried upon the river,
And robbed poor men of their goods;
They robbed and did much shame,
And ever bore the Englishmen the blame.
Now, Jesus save all England
And bless it with His holy hand. Amen

BARBOUR'S BRUCE
THE PURSUIT OF KING ROBERT

*How John of Lorne sought the good King Robert
with the sleuthhound*

The King towards the woods has gone,
Weary, spoiled with sweating and despairing of hope;
Into the woods soon he entered,
And kept himself down towards the vale
Where through the woods ran a stream.
Thither in great haste went he then
And began to rest himself there,
And said he might [go] no farther.
His man said, "Sir, that may not be;
[If] ye abide here, you shall soon see
Five hundred yearning to slay thee,
And they are many against us two;
And since we may not deal with might,
[Let] us help [ourselves] all that we may, with sleight."
The King said, "Since you desire so,
Go forth and I shall go with thee.
But I have heard often said,
That who besides a stream ever
Would wade a bow-draft, he should make
Both the sleuthhound and his leader
Lose the track men made him take;
Prove we if it will do so now,
For was yon devil hound away,
I cared not of the rest, by my faith."
   As he devised, they have done,

And entered into the water soon
And held their way alongside of it;
And after they went onto the land
And held their way as they had before.
And John of Lorne with great haste,
Came with his army right to the place
Where that his five men were slain.
He moaned them when he saw them,
And said after a little time,
That he should avenge their blood in haste;
But other ways the sport went.
There he would make no more dwelling,
But forth in haste follow the King;
Right to the brook they passed before;
But the sleuthhound made pause there,
And waded a long time to and fro
That he could go in no certain way.
Until at the last, John of Lorne
Perceived the hound had lost the track
And said, "We have lost this trouble;
To pass farther may avail nothing,
For the woods are both broad and wide
And he is well far by this time.
Therefore I advise we turn back,
And waste no more work in vain."
With that he rallied his men,
And he took his way to the army.

  Thus escaped the noble King;
But some men say his escaping,
It happened in another way
Than through the wading; for they tell
That the King had a good archer,
And when he saw his King so stand

So that he was left so alone,
He ran on foot always by him
Until he was gone into the woods;
Then said he to himself alone,
That he would make arrest right there
To see if he might slay the hound.
For if the hound might last in life,
He knew full well that they would drive on
The King's track until they took him;
Then he knew well that they would kill him.
And because he would help his lord,
He put his life in jeopardy,
And stood lurking in a bush
While that the hound came to his hand,
And with one arrow soon slew him
And through the woods after withdrew himself.
But whether his escaping happened
As I first told or now I tell
I know it well without lying,
At the brook, the King escaped.
   The King has taken his way forth,
And John of Lorne again is gone
To Sir Amer [de Valence,] that from the chase
With his men was then returning,
That little prospered in their chasing;
For although they made the following
Very eagerly, they won but small;
Nearly all their foe escaped.
Men say Sir Thomas Randall then,
Chasing, the King's banner won,
Wherethrough in England with the King
He had rightly great esteem and love.
When the pursuers were rallied

And John of Lorne had met them there,
He told Sir Amer all the case,
How that the King had escaped,
And how that he slew his five men
And after he drew him into the woods.
When Sir Amer heard this, in haste
He signed himself for the miracle,
And said, "He is greatly praised too,
For I know none that is living
That at mischief can help himself so;
I believe he should be hard to slay,
If he was challenged [to fight] on even terms.
In this case spoke Sir Amer.

And the good King held forth his way,
He and his man, ever while that they
Were passing through the forest.
After they were entering into a wasteland
That was both high and long and broad;
And before they had passed half through it,
They saw on the side three men coming
Like to light armed men and loitering.
Swords they had and axes also,
And one of them upon his neck
A great bare sheep bound.
They met the King and saluted there;
And the King returned to them their salutation
And asked them whither they would [go.]
They said, "They sought Robert Bruce
To meet with him if that they might;
They wished to make their dwelling with him."
The King said, "If that you will so,
Hold forth your way with me,
And I shall make you see him soon."

They perceived by his speaking,
And his behavior, he was the King,
And changed countenance and manner,
And held not in the first attitude;
For they were foes of the King,
And thought to come to treacherous relation,
And dwell with him while that they saw
Their time and bring him out of day.
They agreed to his speech therefore;
But the King who was witty
Perceived well by their behavior
That they loved him in no way.
He said, "Fellows, you men all three,
Until that we are better acquainted
All go by yourselves before us,
And we two certainly in the same [way]
Shall follow you very close behind."
Quote they, "Sir, there is no need
To believe any ill of us."
"None do I," said he, "but I wish
That you go before us until we
Are better known to [each] other."
"We grant [it,]" they said, "since you wish so."
And forth upon their way began to go.

   Thus they went until the night was near,
And when the first was come
To an empty husband's house and there
They slew the sheep which they bore,
And struck a fire for to roast their meat,
And asked the King if he would eat
And rest himself until the meat was prepared.
The King who was hungry, I promise,
Assented to their speech in haste;

But he said he wished alone
To be with himself and his fellow
At a fire, and they all three
At the [other] end of the house should make
Another fire; and they did so.
They drew themselves to the [other] end of the house,
And half the sheep sent to them;
And they roasted their meat in haste,
And fell [down] right boldly in order to eat.
   The King well long he had fasted,
And had made very much labor;
Therefore he ate right eagerly.
And when he had eaten hastily,
He had so great a desire to sleep
That he might not sit to think thereto;
For when the veins are filled,
The body becomes heavy evermore,
And the heaviness draws to sleep.
The King who was all tired out,
Saw that sleep had become necessary for him;
To his foster brother he said,
"May I trust you to watch me
Until I take a little sleep?"
"Yes, Sir," he said, "as long as I may endure."
The King then slept a little while,
And slept not but specially
Looked up often suddenly;
For he had fear of the three men,
Who at the other fire were then;
That they were his foe he knew,
Therefore he slept as a bird on the branch.
   The King slept but little then,
When such a sleep fell on his man

So that he might not hold open his eyes,
But fell asleep and he snored.
Now is the King in real peril,
For slept he so, a little while,
He shall be dead before dread;
For the three traitors took good care
That he and his man were asleep.
In very great haste, they got themselves up,
And drew their swords hastily,
And went towards the King in haste
When that they saw he slept so,
And thought they would slay him sleeping.
To him they went in a very great pace,
But in that time, through God's grace,
The King woke up quickly
And saw his man sleeping by him,
And saw the three traitors coming.
Promptly he got to his feet,
And drew his sword out and met them;
And as he went he set his foot
Upon his man very heavily.
He awoke and got up all dizzily;
For the sleep overcame him so
That, before he got up, one of them
Who came in order to slay the King
Gave him a blow in his getting up,
So that he might help him [the King] no more.
The King was so straightly standing there,
That he was never yet standing so;
Was it not for the armor that he had
He had been dead without doubt.
But not therefore in such a way
He helped himself so in the bargain,

That those three traitors he has slain,
Through God's grace and his manhood.
His foster brother was dead there;
Then was he wounded with despairing hope
When he saw he was left alone.
His foster brother he moaned,
And cursed all the other three,
And after took his way himself alone
And rightly to the appointed place has gone.
   The King went forth, wrathful and angry,
Moaning his man very tenderly,
And held his way all by himself alone,
And right to the house is gone
Where he set an appointed place to meet his men.
It was well late of night by then;
He came soon into the house and found
The good wife sitting on the bench.
She asked him soon who he was,
And whence he came and where he was going.
"A traveling man, dame," said he,
"That travels here through the country."
She said, "All that are traveling,
On account of one, are welcomed here."
The King said, "Good dame, what is it
That makes you have such specialty
For men who travel?" "Sir, by my faith,"
Quote the good wife, "I shall tell you;
Good King Robert Bruce is he,
Who is rightly lord of this country.
His foes hold him now in durance
But I think before any thing long to see
Him lord and King over all the land,
So that no foe shall withstand him."

"Dame, love you him so well?" said he.
"Yes, Sir," said she, "as God sees me."
"Dame," he said, "lo, hear him by thee,
For I am he." "Say you truly?"
"Yes, indeed, dame." "And where are gone
Your men, why are you thus alone?"
"At this time, dame, I have no more."
She said, "It may be so in no way;
I have two sons brave and hardy,
They shall become your men in haste."
     As she devised, they have done;
His sworn men become they soon.
The wife made him soon sit and eat;
But he had a short while at the meat
Sitting, when he heard great stamping
About the house; then without thinking,
They started up to defend the house.
But soon after the King recognized
James of Douglas; then was he glad,
And commanded the doors to be opened quickly,
And they came in, all as they were.
Sir Edward Bruce was there,
And James also of Douglas,
Who had escaped from the chase
And met with the King's brother.
After to the tryst that was set for them
They sped themselves with their company,
That was one hundred and fifty,
And when they too had seen the King,
They were joyful of their meeting
And asked how he had escaped;
And he told them all the whole affair,
How the five men pursued him fast,

And how he passed through the water,
And how he met three thieves,
And how sleeping he should [have] been slain,
When he awoke through God's grace;
And how his foster brother was
Slain, he told them all wholly.
Then they all loved God in common,
That their lord had escaped so.

THE POEMA MORALE, OR MORAL ODE

I am older than I was in winter and in learning;
I wield more than I did, my intelligence ought to be more.
Well long have I been a child in word and also in deed;
Although I am old in winter, too young I am in advice.
A useless life have I led and yet I seem to lead myself;
When I think of myself, well sorely I fear for myself.
Almost all I have done in idleness and childishness;
Well late have I thought of myself, but God's mercy acts
    for me.

Many idle words have I spoken, since I could speak,
And many young deeds done that I think of now.
All too often I have been at fault, in work and also in words.
All too much have I spent, too little laid in hoard.
Almost all that I liked before, now it dislikes me;
Who follows his will much, deceives himself.
I might have done better, had I happiness then;
Now I would but I may not, because of age and illness;
Age has overtaken me before I knew it;
I might not see before me because of vapor and mist.
We are cowardly to do good, and in evil all too bold;
A man stands in more fear of men than he does of Christ.
Who does not well the while he may, well often it shall
    rob him.

Then shall they cut down and reap, where they sowed
    before.
Also do good to whom you must, the while you are in life;
No man hopes too much for [his] child and for [his] wife;
Who forgets himself for [his] wife or for [his] child,

He shall come to an evil place, but God be gentle to him.

Send also some good before him, the while he may [get] to Heaven;

Better is an alms before, than be seven after

Be thee not dearer to thy maid nor thy kinswomen than to thyself,

Foolish is [he] who is a friend to other men better than to his own [self.]

The wife hopes not for her husband, nor husband for his wife;

Every man is for himself, the while he is alive

Wise is [he] who thinks of himself, the while he might live,

For soon will the stranger and friendly forget him.

Who did not well the while he might, he shall not when he would;

Many men have sorely worked often disloyally.

No man should put off nor neglect to do well;

For many men promise well, who soon forget it.

The man who wishes to be sure to have God's bliss,

Does well himself while he may when he has [life] certainly.

The rich man thinks to be secure, through wall and through ditch;

He puts his in a secure place who sends them to the heavenly kingdom;

For there is no need to be afraid of fire nor of thief;

There may they not, the hateful nor the pleasant, take [anything] away;

There he has no need to care for wife nor for child.

Thither we send and bear self too little and too seldom;

Thither we should draw and do well often and very frequently,

For there no man shall take anything away from us, with wrong judgment.

Thither we should earnestly draw, would ye believe me,
For there may neither the king nor the judge take it away
    from you.
That best which we had, thither we should send,
For there we might find it afterwards and have without end.
He who did here any good, to have God's favor,
All of it he shall find there, and a hundredfold more.
The one who will hold his possessions well, the while he
    may in this world,
He gives for God's love, then in death he is well held.
Our trouble and our labor is often remained to no avail;
But what we do for the love of God, afterwards we shall
    find it.
No evil shall be unatoned for, nor any good unrequited;
Evil we do all too much, and good less than we should.
He who does most for good now, and he who the least of
    evil,
Either too little and too much, both shall seem to him
    afterwards.
There men shall weigh our works before the Heavenly King,
And give us reward for our labors according to our merits.
Ever each man with them who have, may buy the heavenly
    kingdom,
The one who has more, and [the one] who [has] less, both
    may alike;
So all with his penny as the other with his pound;
That is the most wonderful goods that any man ever found,
And the one who may not do more, [may do] with his
    intention,
As well as who has many pieces of gold;
And often God shows more favor to them who give Him
    less;
All His works and His ways are mercy and righteousness.

Little lacking is God's love, which comes of good will,
And easily esteemed a great gift when the heart is ill.
Heaven and earth He cares for, His eyes are so bright;
Sun, moon, day and fire are dark against His light.
There is nothing concealed or hidden from Him, so great
    is His might;
There is nothing done so secretly nor in such a dark night.
He knows what all people alive do and think,
There is no such lord as is Christ, no king such [as] Our
    Lord.
Heaven and earth and all that is seen is in His hand,
He does all that is His will, on water and on land.
He made the fishes in the sea, and the birds in the air;
He keeps and rules all things and He created all creatures.
He is the beginning without beginning, and end without
    end;
He alone is ever in each place, goes where you go;
He is above us, and beneath, before and behind;
He who does the will of God, also he may find Him.
Each secret He hears and He knows all deeds;
He sees through each man's thought which shall advise
    us too.
We who break God's laws and sin so frequently,
What shall we do or say at the great judgment?
When loving unright then and leading an evil life,
What shall they say or do where angels are terrified?
What shall we bear before us, with whom shall we please,
We who never did good for the Heavenly judge?
There shall be devils so many who will accuse us;
They have forgotten nothing of all that they saw.
All that we misdid here, it shall be known there,
Except we have remedied it the while we are here;
They have all in their writing book what we misdid here;

Though we know them not nor see, they were our com-
        panions.
What shall adulterers do, the deceivers, the perjurers?
Why are so many called, [why] so few chosen?
Why, why were they bought, to what were they born,
Who shall be judged to death and lost [for] evermore?
Each man shall there accuse him and each shall judge him;
His own works and thoughts he shall bring forth to witness;
No man may judge him all so well nor so rightly
For no one knows him so well except only the Lord.
Each man knows himself best, his works and his will;
He who knows least, he often says most, he who knows all
        is quiet.
There is no witness all so great as man's own heart;
Whosoever says that he be whole, himself knows best his
        grief.
Each man shall judge himself to death or to life;
The witness of his works to others, this shall drive him.
All that each man has ever done after he came to man's
        estate,
So it is written in the book, he shall think then;
But the Lord judges not any man after his beginning,
But all his life shall be such as his ending is;
But if the end is evil, all of it is evil, and good if then is
        good.
God grant that our end be good and the wit that he lent us.
    The man who will do no good, not ever lead a good life
Before death and judgment comes to his door, he may
        sorely dread
That he must then not ask grace for it happens frequently;
Therefore he is wise who repents and prays and beseeches
        before the judgment.
When death is at his door, well late he asks for grace;

Well late he leaves evil works that he may do no more.
Sin leaves thee and thou [do it] not when you have no
 strength to do any more;
Therefore he is foolish who so awaits to have God's grace.
Nevertheless, we believe it well, for the Lord Himself said
 it,
At which time so ever that man repents of his misdeeds,
Either later or quickly, he shall obtain mercy;
But he who has not repented anything, very great shall he
 repent.
Many men say, "Who cares for pain that shall have no end?
Pray I for nothing better [than] to be delivered from the
 fetters on Judgment Day?
Little knows he what pain is, and little he knows
What heat has remained there for the soul, how bitter the
 wind blows there;
Had he been there one day, or happen to bear two,
He would not for all the world remain there the third.
What you have seen happen then, you know it certainly,
Evil [it] is to suffer seven years for seven nights of bliss,
Ends our bliss that has ended in everlasting pain.
Better is dirty water drunk than poison mingled with wine;
Roasted pigs are very sweet, as is [the meat] of wild
 animals,
But all too dear he buys them who give therefore his neck.
A full stomach may lightly speak of hunger and of fasting;
So may [those] of pain who know nothing how pain shall
 endure.
Had he been tempted some hours, he would say all other-
 wise;
Lightly esteemed to him were wife and child, sister and
 father and brother;
Ever he would live here in woe and in misery

With them, who might flee from and shun Hell's pains.

Lightly esteemed by him were all worldly wealth and all
earthly happiness.

For to come to the great happiness is happiness with
certainty.

LAYAMON'S BRUT
ARTHUR'S LAST BATTLE

Then came there at one time a valiant man riding,
And brought tidings to Arthur, the King
From Modred, his sister's son; to Arthur he was welcome
Because he thought that he brought very good news.
Arthur lay all night long and spoke with this young knight;
Yet never would he tell him the truth how it went.
When it was day in the morning and the nobility went
    stirring,
Then Arthur got up and stretched his arms;
He got up and sat down for he was very sick.
Then a fair knight asked him, "Lord, how have you fared
    tonight?"
Arthur then answered—for courage was difficult to him—
"Tonight in my sleep where I lay in the bower,
A dream appeared to me; therefore I am very sorry.
[There] appeared in dream to me that a man raised me
    upon a hall;
Then I went bestriding the hall as I would ride;
All the land that I have, all I there observed,
And Gawain sat before me, my sword he bore in his hand.
Then came Modred there going with immeasurable people;
He bore in his hand a strong battle axe;
He began to hew very handily;
And then cut down the posts that held up the hall.
Then I saw Genevere also, to me the loveliest of women;
All the great roof of the hall, she destroyed with her hands.
Then the hall began to tip, and I toppled to the ground,

So that my right arm broke; then said Modred, "Have
    that."
Adown fell the hall and Gawain began to fall,
And fell to the earth; both his arms broke.
And I grasped my dear sword with my left hand,
And smote at Modred's head so that it went on the field;
And the queen also I cut in two with my dear sword,
And afterwards I set her down in a dark pit;
And all my rich people set to flight,
That I knew not under Christ where they were going.
But I myself went to stand upon a woodland,
And I wandered there again widely around that wasteland,
There I saw vultures and horrible birds.
Then came a golden lion traveling over the dunes,
Animals very gracious that Our Lord made.
The lion came running to me and seized me by the middle,
And forth she began to move and go to the sea;
And I saw the waves driven in the sea,
And the lion went into the flood widely with myself.
When we came into the sea then the waves took me away
    from her;
There came a fish traveling and ferried me to land;
Then I was all wet and weary from sorrow and sick.
When I began to awake, I began to shake greatly;
Then I began to tremble as I burnt all [with] fire.
And so I have greatly thought all night about my dream,
For I know certainly gone is all my happiness;
For all my life I must endure sorrow.
Alas, that I have not here Genevere my queen!"
    Then the knight answered, "Lord, you have [it] wrong;
I should never explain the dream with sorrow.
You are the richest man who rules the land,
And the wisest of all who live under the sky,

If it happened, Our Lord willed it not so,
That Modred, your sister's son, had taken your queen,
And all thy royal land set in his own hands,
That you delivered to him when you appeared at Rome,
And he had done all this with his treachery,
Then you might yet avenge thyself worthily with weapons,
And after hold thy land and have power over thy people,
And thy fiend fallen, who wishes evil,
And slay them all clean so that there remained none."

   Then Arthur answered, the noblest King of them all,
"Long be [it] ever that I never think
That ever Modred, my relative, who is the dearest man to
     me,
Would deceive me for all my realm,
Nor Genevere my queen fail in thanks;
It will not begin for any man in the world."

   According to the forthright word then the knight an-
     swered:
"I say the truth, dear King, for I am thy subject,
Thus has Modred done; he has taken thy queen,
And thy pleasant land sets in his own hands.
He is King and she is queen; of thy coming no one knows,
For they never thought in truth that you [would] return
     from Rome.
I am thy own man and saw this treachery;
And I am come to thyself to tell you the truth.
My head be the security [for] what I have said to you,
Truth without falsehood of your dear queen,
And of Modred, thy sister's son, how he has taken England
     from thee."

   Then it remained all still in Arthur's hall;
Then was there sorrow for the good King;
Then were British men very timid for thee.

Then after a time a commotion stirred;
Widely might men hear Britons shout,
And began to tell in many kinds of narratives
How they would condemn Modred and the queen,
And destroy all the people who held with Modred.

Then Arthur called, the most gracious Briton of all,
"Sit down quiet, knights in the hall,
And I will tell you unknown narratives.
Now tomorrow when it is day and the Lord sent it,
I shall go forth into Britain;
And Modred will I slay and burn the queen,
And I will destroy all who delighted in this treachery.
And here I will leave the dearest man to me,
Howell, my dear relative, the highest of my kin,
And half of my army, I leave in this land
To hold all this kingdom that I have in my hand.
And when this thing is all done, I will [go] again to Rome,
And deliver my pleasant land to Gawain, my relative,
And execute my promise after with my bare life;
All my enemies shall make the fated journey."

Then up stood Gawain himself who was Arthur's relative,
And said these words; the earl was made angry:
"Almighty God, Ruler of judgment,
Protector of all the world, why has it happened
That my brother Modred has done this destruction?
Ah, today I disown him here before this nobility,
And I will condemn him with the will of the Lord;
I myself will hang him to be highest of all;
I will destroy the queen with God's law as with horses.
For I am never happy the while she is alive,
And that I have my uncle avenged with the best."
Then the Britons answered with bold voice,
"All our weapons are ready; now we shall go tomorrow."

In the morning when it was day, and the Lord [had]
    sent it,
Arthur himself went forth with his noble people;
Half of them he left and half of them [he] led forth.
Forth he went through the land so that he came to Wissant;
Ships he soon had, many and well furnished;
But for fourteen full nights there lay the army
Waiting for the weather, deprived of wind.
    Now was some cowardly soldier in Arthur's army;
Immediately as he heard the judgment of Modred's death,
He took a servant in haste and sent [him] to the land,
And sent word to Genevere how it was going,
And how Arthur was on the journey with a great army,
And how he would take on, and all how he would do.
The queen came to Modred who was the dearest man to
    her
And told him the news of Arthur the King,
How he would take on and all how he would do.
Modred took his messenger and sent [him] to the land of
    the Saxons.
To Childrich—this King was very powerful—
And asked him to come to Britain; thereof he should
    enjoy [it.]
Modred bade Childrich, the strong and the powerful,
Widely send messengers to the four parts of the land of the
    Saxons,
And bid the knights all that they might obtain;
So that they came soon to this kingdom,
And he would give Childrich of his kingdom,
All beyond the Humber, for he should help him
To fight with his uncle, Arthur, the King.
    Childrich soon went into Britain.
Then Modred had his army assembled from the men
Who were there told sixty thousand

Hardy warriors of heathen people.

Then they were come hither for Arthur's harms,

Modred to help, the most knavish of men.

When the army was assembled from each [part of] mankind,

Then they were there in a heap of one hundred thousand,

Heathen and Christian, with King Modred.

Arthur lay at Wissant; fourteen nights appeared too long to him.

And Modred knew all what Arthur would do there;

Each day came messengers to him from the King's court.

Then it happened at one time, great rains began to rain on him,

And the wind began to turn for him and remained from the eastward;

And Arthur prepared to the ships with all his army,

And commanded that the shipmen bring him to Romney,

There he thought to go up into the land.

When he came to that haven, Modred was opposite to him;

As the day began to dawn, they began to fight

All that long day; many men lay dead there.

Some they fought on the land, some by the shore;

Some they let out of the ships with flying sharp spears.

Gawain went before and enlarged their way,

And slew there quickly eleven soldiers;

He slew Childrich's son, he was come there with his father.

To rest went the sun; sorrow was to the men.

There was Gawain struck down and finished in life,

By a Saxon Earl—sad was his soul.

Then was Arthur sad and sorrowful in heart therefore;

And proclaimed these words, the most powerful Briton of all:

"Now I have lost my dear servants.

I knew by my dream what sorrow was given to me.

Slain is Angel, the King who was my own darling,
And Gawain my sister's son—woe is me that I was born
    man.
Upon the ships now remain my valiant warriors."
    Even these words turned to fight
Sixty thousand anon, good soldiers,
And broke Modred's band, and [he] was well nearly taken
    himself.
Modred began to flee and his people went after;
Fleeing fiendlike, the fields trembled also;
The stones babbled with streams of blood.
There were all who did battle, but that night came too
    quickly;
If the night was not, they were all slain.
The night scattered them around the grasslands and around
    the dunes;
And Modred came forth so that he was at London.
The citizens heard how it was all going,
And denied his going in and all his people.
Modred went then towards Winchester,
And they received him and all his men.
And Arthur went after with all his strength,
So that he came to Winchester with a great army,
And besieged the whole town; and Modred waited therein.
    When Modred saw that Arthur was so near to him,
Often he thought to himself what he might do.
Then in that same night he ordered all his knights,
With all their weapons to go out of the town,
And said that he would stand there with fighting.
He promised the townspeople ever more free laws,
With the [provision] that they help him with greater needs.
When it was daylight, they were ready for their fight.
    Arthur observed that, the King was angry;

He let the trumpets be blown and commanded the men to
    fight;
He commanded all his soldiers and his noble knights
Soon to fight together and to destroy his enemies,
And to destroy all the town and to hang those townspeople.
They stepped together and fought fiercely.

    Modred then thought what he might do;
And he did there as he did elsewhere,
Treachery with the most; for ever he did wickedly;
He deceived his companions before Winchester,
And permitted himself to call immediately his dearest
    knights,
And all his dearest friends and all of his people,
And stole from the fight—the devil take him—
And allowed all the good people there to perish.
[They] fought all day; thinking that their lord lay there,
And they were quickly at much need.
Then he held his way that lay towards Southampton,
And held towards the haven, the most cowardly of warriors;
And took all the ships that were back there,
And the pilots all necessary for the ships,
And went into Cornwall, the most cowardly King in that
    day.

    And Arthur at Winchester beset that town very firmly;
And slew all the people—there was sorrow enough—
The young and the old, all he killed.
When the people were all dead, the town all burnt down,
Then he, with all, thought to burst asunder all the walls.
Then it was happened there what Merlin said once:
"Poor are you, Winchester, the earth shall swallow thee
    up."
So said Merlin, the wise man was famous.

    The queen lay at York, she was never so sad;
That was Genevere, the queen, fairest of women.

She heard said in true words,
How often Modred fled and how Arthur reached him;
Woe was to her there while that she was alive.
Out of York by night she went,
And towards Caerleon as quickly as she might.
Thither two of her knights brought her by night;
And men covered her head with a holy veil,
And she was there a nun, the most careful wife.
Then men knew not of their queen where she was gone,
Many years after it was not known by men in truth,
Whether she was dead and how she went hence,
Whether she had sunk herself into the water.

Modred was in Cornwall and assembled many knights;
To Ireland he sent quickly his messengers;
To the land of the Saxons he quickly sent his messengers;
He called them all at once to come who desired to have
    land,
Or silver, or gold, or anything, or land;
In every way he guarded himself
As did each wise man who came over in need.

Arthur heard that, angriest King,
That Modred was in Cornwall with a great band of men,
And there would remain until Arthur came riding.
Arthur sent messengers around all his kingdom,
And demanded all to come who were alive in the land,
Who were able to fight, to bear weapons;
And whosoever neglected it that the King commanded,
The King would burn him all quickly on the spot.
There moved towards the court unnumbered people,
Riding and going as the rain falls down.
Arthur went to Cornwall with a united army.
Modred heard that and held opposite to him
With unnumbered people—there were many doomed.

Upon the Tamar [River,] they drew together;

Which place is called Camelford, evermore lasted that
same word;

And at Camelford was assembled sixty thousand,

And more thousands thereto; Modred was their chief.

Then thitherward began to ride Arthur the powerful,

With unnumbered people, doomed as they were.

Upon the Tamar [River,] they drew together;

Raised the standards of the armies, held together;

Locked long swords, placed on helmets;

Fire sprang out, spears made noise;

Shields began to break, arrows burst asunder;

There fought all together unnumbered people.

The Tamar was in flood with immeasurable [amounts of]
blood;

A man in that fight might not recognize there any soldier,

Not who did worse, not who better, the conflict was so
mingled;

For each slew right adown, were he soldier, were he knight.

There was Modred slain and finished in life,

And all his knights slain in that battle.

There were slain all the active,

Arthur's retainers, high and low,

And all the Britons of Arthur's table,

And all the foster children of many kingdoms,

And Arthur wounded with a broad battle spear;

He had fifteen fierce wounds;

A man might in the least [of the wounds] press two gloves.

Then was there no more to remain in the fight

Of the two hundred thousand men who lay there hewed
to pieces,

Except Arthur, the King, alone, and two of his knights.

Arthur was wounded, such a wonder.

There came to him a boy who was of his knowing;
He was Cador's son, the earl of Cornwall;
Constantine was named the boy, he was dear to the King.
Arthur looked at him where he lay on the ground,
And said these words with a sorrowful heart:
"Constantine, you are welcome, you were Cador's son;
I assign thee here my kingdom,
And keep my Britons one to the end of your life,
And hold them to all customs that have stood in my days
And all the good customs that stood in Uther's days.
And I will go to Avalon, to the fairest maiden of all,
To Argante, the queen, the very beautiful fairy,
And she shall make my wounds all sound,
Make me all whole with a consecrated drink;
And afterwards I will come to my kingdom,
And live with the Britons with great joy."
Just as the words went, there came upon the sea [a thing]
That was a short boat gliding moving by the waves,
And two women therein, wonderfully dressed;
And they took Arthur anon, and quickly carried him,
And softly laid him down and began to glide forth.
Then it happened what Merlin said once
That great care was to be taken at Arthur's departure;
Britons believe yet that he is alive,
And lives in Avalon with the fairest fairy of all;
And the Britons ever yet look [for the time] when Arthur
        comes gliding [back.]
There never was the man born of any woman chosen
Who could say more of the truth of Arthur;
Except what was [said] by a wise man, called Merlin;
He announced with words—his speech was true—
That an Arthur shall yet come to help the English.

THE LIFE OF SAINT JULIANA

For the love of Our Lord which is the Father of creation and in His dear Son's name and of the Holy Ghost that proceeds from them both, [this work is made for] all unlearned men who are not able to understand to listen to the Latin tongue and [who can] listen to a maiden's way of life which is turned into English from Latin so that the holy Lady in Heaven [might] love us the more, and from this lying life lead us with her intercession, who are chosen by Christ, into the eternity of Heaven.

This maiden and this martyr was Juliana called by name in Nichomedes town and came from a heathen family and her natural father was called Africanus, the greatest of heathens. Those who were Christians, he cruelly dragged them to death, and she as they whom the Heavenly Father loved, left all her old customs and began to love the living Lord, the lovable God who knows and rules all that is in the world and all that is made.

There was in that time, as readings tell, Maximian, the proud emperor in Rome, raising high and praising heathen idols with great unmeasured retinue and unavailing honor and condemning all those who believed in the Lord. This Maximian loved a man of the race and also rich from rents, Eleusius was [he] called, and [they] were also fellows through much friendship. This maiden's father and he [Eleusius] were very well together. As he sometimes saw her, an exceptionally fair and a friendly youth, he felt himself wounded so that, without remedy of her, he might not live. Africanus knew well that he [Eleusius] was free born and that [she] would become a free born woman with him and

granted his daughter to him; and soon she was wholly be-
trothed against her will. And she trusted in Him, and each
day's dawn [she] went to Church to learn God's teaching,
earnestly to know how she might best keep her purity and
her maidenhood without marriage to man. Eleusius, who
loved her, it seemed long to him that this deed was done
that she be brought to bed in wedlock. And as she thought
some ways for herself to escape, sent to him saying that she
would not alight so humbly nor draw near to him for any
living man until he was the highest under Maximian in
Rome, that is, the prefect. Soon as he [Eleusius] heard this,
he obtained from the emperor [his request] that he grant
him to become a reeve as he had desired; and he, as men
then loved, did lead him into the chariot that the rich ride
in and take him through town from street to street. And
also the chariot that he was in was covered with purple,
with costly cloth and with ciclatoun and precious cloth as
they who have high [priced] things to guard. And when
he had done this, he sent to her saying that he had worked
her will and she should do his.

Juliana, the fair one, the dear one of Jesus Christ, em-
boldened herself by His blissful love, sent an answer to him
by one of her messengers; "Eleusius, know you it well prepared, be angry as thou [wilt] be angry, I no longer desire
to conceal it from thee; if you will leave the laws that you
belong to and believe in God, the Father and in His
precious Son and in the Holy Ghost, I will indeed take
thee; if you will not, you are averse to me and seek thee
another love." When the reeve heard this, he became very
angry and called her father and took on to tell him how his
daughter dragged him from day to day and after that he
thought to have his will, she sent him those words so
strangely. "By that same God," said her father, "That man
is loath to anger, be it true as you said, to heal thy anger,

she said it; and now I will, in all great anger, deliver her
to thee to work thy will and all that you indeed like as with
thy own." And the man called her forth before her father,
and he took fairly to testing his daughter: "My precious
daughter, wherefore forsake you thy victory and thy felicity
and thy happiness and the joy that would awaken and grow
from thy wedlock to which I advise thee? For he is lord
enough, Eleusius, in Rome, and you might be a lady,
daughter, if you indeed will." Juliana, the fair one, answered him and said as they who have hope in their God,
"If he will believe in Almighty God, then may he speak
thereof and prosper quickly enough; and if he will not, [he]
shall not marry me, marry where his will is." When her
father heard this, then he took to swearing: "By my royal
lord, Apollo, and by my dear lady, Diane, whom I love
much, if you hold hereon, I will let animals tear [thee] to
pieces and tear thee asunder and give thy flesh to the birds
of the air." Juliana answered him and softly said, "Think
you not, dear father, that you frighten me so, for Jesus
Christ, God's Son, whom I believe in and love as the most
lovable Lord in life, though I be burnt and torn to pieces
limb from limb, I will not be obedient to thee." Then her
father again took on with gentleness to try, if he might in
any way, know her heart and said to her lovingly that she
should not wish for any pleasure [ever so] lightly that he
should not obtain it [for her,] with which she would show
her gratitude. "No," said the maiden, "shall I put myself
from Him who is delivered from all devils and judged to
each death, to perish with him world without end, for his
wedlock's happiness or for any joy? Forsooth, I say it,
unworthy it is of me. I wish that he knows it well and you
also with him that I am wedded to One that I desire truly
to hold and to love without falsehood which is unlike him
and all worldly men. I wish neither to leave Him nor

prevaricate for felicity nor joy, for woe nor for pleasure, that you might give to me."

Then her father took to [being] very fearfully angry and asked very sorrowfully, "But what is He, this man whom you are wedded to, to whom you have lent your love without me for whom you think little of [and] whom you should love? I never as I know was known to Him." "For God," quote the maiden, "thy harm is the more; not because that you have often heard of Him already, who is Jesus, God's Son who, in order to deliver mankind who should be lost, gave up His dear life on the cross. I never saw Him, of that I repent sorely; and I love Him and believe as in the Lord, neither devil nor man shall remove me from Him." "For my life," quote her father, "You shall be hateful of His love for you shall be beaten with rods so severely that you shall be a woman become to bad health." "So much," quote she, "I become the dearer to Him as I endure the more painful things for His love. What thy will is, do now." And he ordered quickly to strip her stark naked and to beat her so terribly that her dear body became covered with blood. And also she did bleed so badly that the blood poured down on the rod. And she began to shout, "Beat [me] as you beat, you servant of Belial, you might nohow belittle my love, not my belief towards Him, my lovable dear, my loving Lord; I will not permit your advice which deceives yourself, not your dunghill idols that are the exalted vessels of the fiends, nor praise, because of injury not because of torment that you might do [to me]." "No," quote he, "is it so? It shall become manifest soon for I will deliver thy miserable body to Eleusius, the rich reeve in Rome, and he shall destroy and wrong thee according to his will with all kinds of pains." "You," quote the maiden, "that Christ might reign, for you might do nothing to me except what He permits you, to increase my reward and the

joy that belong to maidenhood; for so ever the more you
injure me here, so [much the more] my crown becomes
brighter and fairer. For I will gladly endure every affliction
for the love of my dear Lord, and softly becomes each
trouble for me when I serve Him; though you will deliver
me to Eleusius. I care not for you either that you might
harm me; for as you harm me the more here, so [much]
more you help me sevenfold to Heaven. And if you put me
to death, it is precious to me, and I shall therethrough
gladly enter into eternal bliss and you shall, wretches,— in
woe, with your worth that you were born [with]—sink for
your evil fortune deeply into Hell to the bitter calamity."

Her father, Africanus, through this bitter vexation,
brought her to Eleusius, the terrible reeve, and he did bring
her before him to his high seat as he sat in judgment as the
reeve of the town. . . And [on her he] set that harmful
beast as a bristly boar that grounded his tusks and took on
to foam and to gnash his teeth at this meek maiden and
thought in which way he might attack her. And [he] did
fetch a vat and fill it with pitch and heat it boiling hot, and
ordered her thrown therein; she called to the Lord and it
cooled immediately, and became for her as pleasant as any
tepid water that was made lukewarm for bathing, and
leaped boiling hot up again for the same [ones] that had
prepared it and scalded completely fifty and ten of them
and destroyed fifty all told. When the reeve saw this, he
tore his clothes and grabbed himself by the hair and took to
abusing his idols and blaming his lord. "Quickly," quote
he, "out of my eyesight so that I see her no more before
the body with the belly be separated from her head."

Soon as she heard this, she praised God in Heaven and
became very glad for what she had wished. Men led her
and moved swiftly, and she was easily pulled. As she
stayed in the place where she should endure death, then

came the same Belial from Hell that she had beaten behind her and began to shout, "Ah, stalwart men, spare
ye nothing, she has done all shame to us; injure her now
and pay her ready security, nor stop ye ever." Juliana, the
fair one, opened her eyes and looked towards him and the
evil one flinched and moved himself backward as a shot
arrow. "Woe is me that I live," quote he, "then I not be
caught now, and if she catches me now, never find I a
physician; [if] she grabs me once, I [shall] never go ever
more." And leaped him backward as a bear, that monster,
he might not think anything. As she was about to stoop and
stretch forth her neck, she prayed first and took on so to
teach them who were there and thus said, "Listen to me,
dear men, and listen only a while. Weep and be sorry for
your sins and lessen [them] with true confession and with
restitution; leave your violations of the law and build your
buildings on a true foundation that fears no wind, nor any
weather either. See that the Heavenly Lord be the foundation of all that you work, for that stands steadfast; falls
what falls. Call earnestly to God in holy church that He
give you intelligence enough for the doing and strength to
you with His strength against the strong monster that seeks
ever and ever in order to swallow you up. Listen to the
written lore and love it thereafter; well is [it] for him that
walks well in the little while and knows himself well and
often groans for his sins. This would turn away as water
that runs, and as an appearing dream vanishes with its
mirth; And all is nothing except a false wind that we live
in. Leave the false and love the true, for we should leave
this life, we never know when, and we reap that ripe seed
that we sowed. Strongly, I beseech you that you pray for
me, brethren and sisters." And kissed them all a kiss of
peace, all as she stood and looked upward and raised her
voice: "Lord, God Almighty, you love true belief; you

leave not to thine foe, thine likeness; ah, receive me to Thee and put me in Thy angelic court with maidens' company. I give my ghost to Thee, Lord." And with that same, bent and sank headlong down to the earth, soon beheaded; and the fair angels, with her soul, singing rose to Heaven.

Soon afterwards came a holy woman called Sophia, by Nichomedes city, on the road towards Rome, begot of a high family, and took this maiden's body and bore it in a boat, dearly wrapped in dear clothes. As she was on the water came up a storm and drove them to land in Compania; and there did Sophia, from the sea a mile, set a church and put her body therein in a stone coffin, with honors as it avails to do for saints. The reeve, when he heard this, began to row after, in order to rob it from them, and in the sea drowned; for the storm arose stark and strong and broke the ship's side, drowned some thirty of them and thereto also four and cast them driven about on the land, where wild animals tore them limb from limb, and the unholy souls sank into Hell.

Thus that fair maiden went through pain to heavenly joy, in that renowned city named Nichomedes, on the sixteenth day of the month of February, the fourteenth day before the first of March that comes after. She intercedes to God for us, for the grace of Himself who rules the Trinity and is one undivided though. Praised and exalted by Himself alone, as He is worthy and ever ought to be, world without end. Amen.

THE ANCREN RIWLE,
OR RULE OF NUNS

Conversation and tasting are both in the mouth as sight is in the eyes; but we shall leave tasting until we speak of your meat, and speak now of conversation and thereafter of hearing, of both together sometimes as go together.

And first of all when you shall [go] to the parlor window, learn and your maidens [also,] who it is that is come, for such it may be that you should excuse yourself; when you all must [go] forth, cross very earnestly your mouth, ears and eyes and the breast also and go forth with God's dread to a priest. And before say "the confiteor," and thereafter "benedicite," what he has to say, hearken to his words and sit all still so that when he departs from you, that he knows not of your good, nor your evil either, not that he knows you to blame or to praise. Some are so well learned and utter words so wisely that they wish that he knows it who sits and speaks to them word for word and becomes a master who should be a nun and teaches him who is come to teach her; [she] desires by her conversation soon to be made known and known with the wise. Known she is well, for through the same thing that she thinks to be held wise, he understands that she is a fool, for she hunts for praise and catches blame. For at the last when he is gone away. "That nun," he will say, "is of much speech." Eve held a long conversation in Paradise with the snake who told her all the lessons that God had taught her and Adam about the apple; and so the fiend through her words understood right away her weakness and found the way to her for her lost condition. Our Lady, Saint Mary, did all in another way and did not tell the angel any story but asked him a thing briefly that she knew not. You, my dear sisters, follow Our Lady and not the cackling Eve. Therefore the nun, whosoever she be, also much as she ever can and may, hold her silence. She has nothing of the hen's nature. When the hen has laid [an egg,] [she] can [do] nothing except cackle. And what does she obtain thereby? Comes the swift eagle right away and robs her of her eggs and eats all that what she should have brought forth, her birds alive. And exactly also the terrible swift eagle, the devil, bears away from the cackling nun and swallows all the good that she has begotten, and should, as the birds bear themselves up towards Heaven, if she had not cackled. The wretched peddlar, he makes more noise to sell his soap, than [does] the rich mercer for all his precious wares. To some holy men whom you be confident of, as you must be of few, good [it] is that you ask advice and the remedy that he teaches you against temptations, and in confession, show him if he will hear your greatest and your most loathsome sins, because that you repent of them, and through the commiseration, cry to Christ inwardly for mercy for yourself and to have you in His mind and in His prayers. "Sed multi veniunt ad vos in vestimentis ovium, intrinsecus autem sunt lupi rapaces"; "But know you and be aware," he said, Our Lord, "for many cometh to you clothed with lamb's fleece and be wild wolves." Worldly men believe few [men,] religious yet less; desire ye not their acquaintance too much. Eve without fear spoke to the snake; Our Lady was afraid of Gabriel's speech.

Without witness of man or of woman, what you might hear, speak ye not to any man often nor long; and though it be of confession in the same house or where he might see towards you, sit thee [with a] third [person,] except if the same third or time be lacking. This is not for you, dear sisters, said, nor for others such; not, because the true is disbelieved and the innocent often calumniated for want of witnesses. Men believe the evil soon, and the miserable gladly tell falsehoods about the good. Some unfortunate, when she said that she confessed herself, has confessed herself all too wonderfully. Therefore the good ought ever to have a witness for two reasons; namely, the one is that the envious might not lie about them so that the witness prove them not false, the other is in order to give the other example and take away from the evil nun that same unfortunate guile that I spoke about.

Out of church windows hold ye no conversation with any person, but bear worship thereto for that holy sacrament that you see therethrough; and take at another time your women to the windows of the house, the other men and women to the windows of the parlor, to speak but for need; you ought not [speak] except at those two windows.

[Keep] silence ever at thy meat, for if other religious do it, as well you know, you ought [to do it] before all; and if any have a dear guest, put the maiden with her as in her place to gladden her companion, and she shall have leave to open her window once or twice and to make signs to her with a glad countenance. Some courtesy is nevertheless turned to evil for her; under semblance of good is often concealed sin. [There] ought to be much between a nun and a house lady. Every Friday of the year hold silence except if it be a double feast and then hold it some other day in the week; in Advent, and on ember-days, Wednesdays and Fridays; in Lent three days and all the Holy Week before noon on Easter eve. To your maidens, you must say though, with few words what you desire, and if any good man is come from afar, hearken to his speech and answer with few words to his asking.

A great fool were he who might for his own profit,

whetherso he would, grind gravel or wheat, if he ground the gravel and left the wheat. Holy speech is wheat as Saint Anslem says. She grinds gravel who chatters. The two cheeks are the grindstones; the tongue is the clapper. Look, dear sisters, that your cheeks grind never except soul-food, nor your ears hearken ever except to the need of the soul; and not only your ears but your windows closed against idle speech, so that to you comes no conversation nor news of the world.

You should for no thing curse nor swear except if you speak evidently or truly or in some such manner; preach you not to any man, nor let any man ask you advice or counsel, nor tell you [any.] Counsel women only. Saint Paul forbade women to preach—"Mulieres non permitto docere." Chastise thee no man, nor blame him for his bad manners, except if he becomes too familiar. Holy old nuns must do it in some ways, but it is not a sure thing [even for them,] let it not happen with the young. There is their master who is set over others and have them to guard; the nun has none to guard except herself and her maidens. Hold each one his own master and rob no others. Many a man thinks to do well who does all for the evil one; for as I said before, under semblance of good is often concealed sin, and through such chastisement, has some nun raised between herself and her priest either a little deceiving love or a much worse thing.

Seneca said, "Ad summam volo vos esse rariloquos, tuncque pauciloquos"; that is, "At the end of the conversation," said Seneca, the wise, "I wish that you spoke seldom and then but little." But many dam up her words in order to let more out, as men do water at the dam of the mill; and so did Job's friends who came to comfort him, sat quiet all week, but when they had all begun to speak, then they never knew to cease their clapper. Gregory:

"Censura silencii nutritura est verbi." So it is with many as
Saint Gregory said, "Silence is word's nurse and brings
forth talk." In another place as he said, "Juge silencium
cogit celestia meditari,—"Long silence and well kept, forces
the thoughts up towards Heaven there." Also as you might
see that water when men dam it and stop [it] well before
so that it might not go downward, then it is necessary for
[it] to climb upward; and you in all these ways dam up
your words and stop your thoughts, as you wish that they
climb and hasten towards Heaven, and not fall downward,
and be dispersed around the world as does much talk. But
when you needs must speak, to few persons release up your
mouth's floodgate as men do at the mill and let down soon.

Of Domestic Matters

It does not become a nun to make herself generous from
other men's alms. Would not men laugh any beggar loudly
to scorn who offered men a feast? Mary and Martha, they
both were sisters, but of their life separated. You nuns have
taken to yourselves Mary's part, that Our Lord Himself
praised, "Maria optimam partem eligit." "Martha, Martha," he said, "you are in great agitation; Mary has chosen
the better [part,] and nothing shall take her part away
from her." Housewifery is Martha's part, and Mary's part
is stillness and rest from all the noise of the world so that
nothing stops her for to hear God's voice. And look what
God said that nothing shall take that part away from you.
Martha has her occupation; let her be, and sit you still
with Mary at God's feet and hearken to Him only. Martha's occupation is to feed and to cloth poor men as a house-
lady: Mary ought not to meddle with her thereof, and if
any blame her, God Himself was wholly for her thereof,
as Holy Scriptures testifies. On the other side, no nun ought
to take except sparingly what is necessary for her. Whereof

then may she make herself generous? She shall live by alms as carefully as she ever may and not gather to give it [away] afterwards. She is not a housewife but is a nun of the church. If she may spare any poor shred, send them secretly out of her dwelling; under semblance of good is often concealed sin. And how shall those rich nuns that are tillers of the earth or have set rents, do secretly their alms for their poor neighbors? Desire not to have the words, of one generous nun, nor for to give much, nor to be greedier in order to have more. Greediness is the root of her bitterness; all are the boughs bitter that spring from her. To ask it in order to give it [away] is not the part of a nun. From a nun's courtesy and from a nun's generosity is often come sin and shame in the end.

Women and children who have worked for you, whatsoever you spare on yourself, make them to eat; [let] no man [eat] before you except he has need, nor invite you to drink anything. I desire not that men account you courteous nuns. From a good friend, take all that you have need for when she offers it to you; but from no body take you anything without need, lest you catch the name of greedy nuns. From a man that you misbelieve, you take neither less nor more, nothing so much as [it] be a ginger root. Much need shall drive you before you ask outright; though show to your dearest friends your misery.

You, my dear sisters, should have no animals except a cat. A nun who has possessions, seems but a housewife as Martha was, than a nun; in no way may she be Mary with the peacefulness of heart. For then must she think of the cows' fodder and of hired herdsmen, flatter the guardian of the hedge, take precautions when men impound her [the cow,] and recompense the harms though. Christ knows this is a loathsome thing when men make complaint in town concerning the nuns' property. Though if any must needs

have a cow, look that she annoys no man, nor harms, nor
that her thoughts be not fastened thereon. A nun ought not
to have anything that draws her heart outward. Let no
trade drive you; a nun that is fond of bargaining, she sells
her soul to the merchant of Hell. Keep ye nothing in your
house of other men's things, nor possessions, nor clothes;
receive ye nothing of Church vestments, nor the chalice;
except if strength makes it necessary or much fear, for from
such caretaking much evil ofttimes has come. Within your
dwelling let no man sleep. If great need for all makes
[people] to break into your house, the while that it be ever
broken into, look that you have therein with you only
women of clean life, night and day.

ROBERT OF GLOUCESTER'S CHRONICLE
HOW THE NORMANS CAME TO ENGLAND

Much has been the sorrow often in England,

As you might here and before heard and understood,

Of many battles that have been and that men took that land.

First, as you have heard, the Emperor of Rome,

Afterwards the Saxons and English with strong battles,

And afterwards they of Denmark who held it so long;

At last they of Normandy, whose dominion is yet here,

Won it and hold it yet, I will tell you in which manner.

   When William the Bastard heard tell of Harold's treachery,

How he had made himself King and with such falsehood,—

For that land was taken by him, as he well knew,

To keep it for him and he well trusted him;—

As the gracious one he acted at first and sent him messengers

So that he understood him better in order to amend his deed

And thought about the great oath that he had made for him before

To keep England well for him and to marry his daughter also,

And held him thereby to the agreement as he promised the King too;

And unless he acted promptly, he would send him other news,

And seek him out before twelve months and win his right,

So that he should not have in all England a nook to keep
  himself in.
  Harold sent to him word that it was foolish to trust
To such oaths as were made with strength as well he knew;
For if a maid plight her troth to do a foolish deed
All alone privately, without her friends' advice,
That promise was for nothing; and more especially it
  ought [to be known] here
That I swore an oath that was all in thy power.
Without counsel of all the land, of things that were not
  mine;
Therefore the oath sworn in necessity, was broken in neces-
  sity.
And if you will seek me in England, you [will] not be so
  stern;
You [may] be sure you shall not find me in any nook.
  When William heard that he would sustain his treachery
He did summons his knights from all Normandy
To advise him in this case, and to help in such need;
And he began to offer them largely from his earnings,
As they found afterwards in England, when it was won;
The better [part] was for him [with] their heart in this case.
William, the Duke, said all his will among them,
That four things made him most begin that deed:
That Godwin, Harold's father, did put to death
So vilely Alfred, his cousin, and his fellows also;
And because Harold had broken his oath that he had
  sworn with his right hand,
That he desired to keep England for his use;
And because Saint Edward gave him England too;
And because he was next of his blood and was best thereto,
And because Harold had no right except in falsehood;
These things made him most begin that deed.
  And because he desired that all men see his faithfulness,

To Pope Alexander he sent to advise him in this case.
Harold's falsehood then the Pope saw there,—
And perchance men told him more than was true,—
The Pope absolved and blessed William and all his
Who should [go] with him into this battle certainly,
And consecrated his banner that men bore before him.
Then was he and all his gladder than they were before,
So that this Duke had his harvest all ready again,
His barons and knights with him, in order to go.

To the haven of Saint Valery, the Duke then went,
With the men that he had and more remained.
After harvest then, their ships and they were all ready,
And [when] the wind came according to desire, they began
    to raise their sails,
And thitherward on the sea very gladly took their way,
So that they came to England besides Hastings;
They thought when they came to land that all was in their
    hands.
As soon as William, the Duke, set his foot on the land
One of his knights cried out, "Hold fast, William, now
To England, for there is no King except you;
For sure you are, England is now thine certainly."
William, the Duke, immediately forbade all his
That there be no one so wild to plunder, nor to do harm
    there in any manner
Upon the land that was his except to them who were against
    him.
For fourteen nights they all remained there about,
And planned the battle and prepared their army.

King Harold sat glad enough at York at his meat,
So that there came a messenger before he had eaten,
And said that William, the Duke, was come to Hastings,
And had raised his banner and taken all the country.
Harold immediately with great heart courageous enough,

As [if] he took account of no man, thitherward drew he fast.
He did not call all his people, so headstrong was he,
And all for him in the other battle fell in so fair circum-
    stances.
When Duke William knew that he was come so near,
A monk he sent him with a message and did the sly one:
That land that was given to him that he should give it up,
[Or they would] come and vindicate the right with swords
    in the field.
If he said that he had no right thereto,
That upon the decision of the Pope in Rome, he should
    rest it,
And he would stand thereto all without fight,
Although Saint Edward gave it to him and although he
    had a right thereto.
Harold sent him word again that he would not take any
    land from him,
Not looking to Rome, but with sword and hand.
When it might not be [any] other [way,] either on his side
Planned and made them [selves] ready to prepare for battle.

The English all the night before firmly began to sing,
And spent all the night in gluttony and drinking.
The Normans did not so but cried to God firmly,
And confessed themselves each after the other while the
    night lasted,
And in the morning they did receive communion with meek
    hearts enough.

And afterwards the Duke with his army drew towards the
    battle,
For a time he began to prepare and counsel his knights;
"You, knights," he said, "who are of so noble deeds,
Who were never overcome, nor your elders any more,

Understand from the King of France that your elders did
    such woe,
How my father in Paris amid his kingdom
With the prowess of your fathers overcame him with
    strength.
Understand how your elders also took the King,
And held him until he had amended what he had misdone;
And Richard who was then a child yielded Normandy,
Who was the Duke here before and that to such mastery
That at each Parliament that he was in France,
That he was gird with sword the while he was there,
Nor that the King of France was his so hardy,
Nor none at the Parliament [was] that bore knife nor sword.
Understand also the deeds that this Richard did also,
That he never overcame any kings alone but well more
    thereto,
But he overcame the devil and cast him down,
Together as they wrestled and bound him fast
Behind at the back; of such prowess you think,
Feel not ashame ye of that Harold who was ever of evil
    trick,
And was foresworn before you that he would with his
    retinue
Turn his stomach towards us and his face in battle.
Understand the treachery that his father and he wrought,
And they that are here with him, when they brought to
    death
So vilely Alfred, my cousin, and my kinsmen also.
How in any way might more shame be done?
Many that did this deed you might see here;
How long shall their evil heads be on their shoulders?
Draw your swords and see who may do best,
That men see your prowess from East to the West,

In order to avenge that gentle blood, that was so vilely
    taken
Of our kinsmen, for we must do well, our time is come."
    The Duke had not said all that with great earnestness
[Before] his people to the battle quickly shot.
A servant who was called Taylerfer went forth there before
And immediately slew an Englishmen who bore the banner,
And eftsoon another banner and the third almost also,
But he himself was slain before the deed was done.
    The first part of his army before Harold with such
    ingenuity
[He] set so thickly that no man might come within,
With strong shields before them so that the archers did
    them no harm,
So that the Normans were brought near to the ground.
William conceived a plan and began to flee fast,
And his people forth with him as they were afraid,
And fled over a long dale and up a hill.
The English army was proud enough when they saw this,
And began to spread themselves and took after this way.
The Normans were above the hill, the others came upward,
And turned on them from above so easily as it would be
    downward,
And the others beneath might not [go] so easily upward,
And they were scattered about before all so that men might
    go between them.
The Normans were then well provided about in each end,
And flung stones adown upon them enough,
And with spears and with arrows slew many of them,
And with swords and axes, for they who went upward,
Might not have any chance for striking as they who came
    down,
And their vanguard was scattered so that men might go
    within them;

So that the Normans slew, on each end, many
Of the English all for nothing, so that the valley was nearly
As a hill, filled with dead men as a hill on a hill.
The bowmen downward, all for nothing, slew many on the
    ground
So that Harold, shot through the eye, was wounded to
    death;
And a knight that saw that he was brought to death
And smote him as he lay beneath and slew him as for
    nothing.
From [the time] that it was in the morning, the battle lasted
    strong
Until it was high mid afternoon and that was somewhat
    long.
Many were the good blows that Duke William gave in a
    day;
For three horses he [had] killed under him as men say,
Spurred violently and wearied by riding and wounded
    badly also,
And broken to pieces against dead men before the battle
    was done;
And yet was William's grace that day so good
That he had no wound wherethrough he shed one drop of
    blood.
    Thus, lo, the English people for nought came to the
    ground,
Because of a false King that had no right to the kingdom,
And came to a new lord who was more in the right;
But his neither, as men may see, was in pure right.
And thus was brought into Normans' hands that land
    indeed,
That [it was] a venture if evermore [there] is recovery
    thereof.
The high men that are in England are of the Normans

And the low men of Saxons, as I understand,
So that you see on either side what right you have thereto;
But I understand that it was done through God's will.
For the while that men of this land were pure heathens,
No land nor people were against them in arms;
But now after that, these people received Christianity
And well little will hold the promises that they took,
And turned to sloth and to pride and to lechery,
To gluttony and highway men much to robbery,
As the ghost in a vision told to Saint Edward,
How there should come such misery into England
For robbery of high men, for adultery of the clergymen,
How God would send sorrow in this kingdom.

 Between Michaelmass and Saint Lucy's to Saint Calixtus
  day,
As fell in this year on a Saturday,
In the year of grace as it happened also;
One thousand and six and sixty were done in battle.
Duke William was then nine and thirty years old,
And one and thirty years was he Duke of Normandy before.
When this battle was done Duke William did put
His fair people, who were slain, into the earth through all
 things.
To [all] that desired [it,] he gave permission that his foe
 be put into the earth;
Harold's mother besought him very earnestly for her son
By messengers and charitably prayed to him for her thing
To grant her her son's body in order to put into the earth.
William sent it [the body] to her fair enough without any
 thing wherefore,
So that it was through her borne with great honor,
To the house at Waltham and brought into the earth then
In the Holy Cross Church that he did raise himself,
A house of religion, of canons certainly.

It was there put into the earth as it is yet.

William, this noble Duke, when he had done all this,
He took his way to London, he and all his
As King and prince of the land with nobility enough.
The people of the town drew to him with a fair procession,
And received him fair enough as King of the land.

Thus came, alas, England into Norman hands;
And the Normans could speak nothing except their own
    speech,
And spoke French as they did at home and did also teach
    their children,
So that high men of this land who come from their blood
Holds all this speech that they took from them;
For except a man knows French, men think little of him
But low men hold to English and to their own speech yet.
I know there is in all the world no country
That holds not to their own speech except England alone.
But men know well for to know both, it is well,
For the more a man knows, the more valuable he is.

OLD KENTISH SERMONS

On The Calming of The Sea

*"Ascendente Ihesu in naviculam, secuti sunt eum dis-
cipuli eius. Et ecce motus factus est magnus in mari ita, ut
operiretur fluctibus. Erat autem illis ventus contrarius."*

We read in the Holy Gospel for today that Our Lord
went one time into a ship and His disciples with Him onto
the sea. And as they were in the ship, so arose a great
tempest of wind; and Our Lord had laid Himself down to
sleep in the ship before this tempest arose. His disciples had
great fear of this storm so [they] awoke Him and said to
Him, "Lord, save us; for we perish." And He knew well
that they had no good belief in Him, then said to them,
"What fear you, people of little faith?" Then Our Lord
rose up and touched the wind and the sea and all so quickly
it was still. And as the men who were in the ship had seen
this miracle, so wondered they much.

This is the fair miracle that the Gospel of today tells us;
therefore, shall our faith be the better strengthened in such
a Lord who may do and does such miracles when He wills.
But it is necessary for us to see that one who succored them
in their peril, who succors us in our needs, so that we call to
Him that He keep us. And He will do it gladly if we beseech Him with good will for mercy, also [He] Himself
said in Holy Scriptures, "Salus populi ego sum, et cetera";
"I am," He said, "the healer of the people; when they call
to Me in their sorrows and in their needs, I succor them and
take from them all their evil without end." We cry out to

Him for mercy, certainly, if the devil will encumber us through sin, through pride, or through envy, or through wrath, or through other manner of deadly sins; cry we out to Him for mercy and we say to Him, "Lord, save us, that we perish not," and so that He will deliver us from all evil and so that He gives us such works to do in this world, so that the souls of us might be saved on Judgment Day and go to the bliss of Heaven. Quod ipse prestare dignetur, etc.

On The Parable of The Vineyard

"Simile est regnum celorum homini patrifamilias qui exiit, primo mane, conducere operarios in vineam suam."

Our Lord God Almighty speaks to us in the Holy Gospel of today and shows us one example that, if we will do His service, that we shall have the very great reward in Heaven. For so says Our Lord in the Gospel for today, that [there] was a goodman who first went out in the morning in order to hire workmen into his vineyard, for one penny by agreement; and as he had made this agreement so he sent them into his vineyard. So did he from nine to twelve and at midday also. When it was again the evening so he came into the market, so he found workmen who were idle. Then said he to them, "Why be ye idle?" And they answered and said, "Lord, for we found none today who hired us." "Go, now," he said, the goodman, "into my vineyard and I shall give you what is right." They went into the vineyard with the others. When that it was well evening, then the lord said to his sergeant, "Call the workmen, and pay them for their labor and begin with them who came last and go through all to the first, give each one of them one penny." The sergeant did the lord's order, so paid the workmen and gave each one a penny. And so they saw they who came in the morning that they who were last come, had every one of them [received] a penny, then they thought to have more. Then they murmured among themselves and said, "Those last have labored one hour and you make them fellows with us that have all day been in the vineyard and have suffered the burden of the pain and of the heat of all the day." Then answered the goodman to one of them: "Friend," he said, "I do thee no wrong. Who dislikes that I do my will." And also Our Lord had told this parable as He said afterwards, "So shall the first be last, and the last first; many are called but few are chosen."

Now hear the significance. This goodman betokens God Almighty, Our Lord. The vineyard betokens the service of Our Lord. The workmen betoken all those who do Christ's service. Then the time of the day betokens the time of the world. By the morning Our Lord hired the workmen into His vineyard when He sent the patriarchs at the beginning of the world into His service, who through good faith served Him and told His teachings to all those whom they had said it to. Also in the morning hours and at midday, He hired the workmen into the vineyard whom He sent at the time that Moses was and Aaron; and in the time of the prophets, He put many good men into His service who through great love for Him, held and did His service. Against the evening, God Almighty hired workmen into His vineyard when that He at last in this world took flesh and blood in the maiden, Saint Mary and showed [up] in this world. Then He found men who all day had been idle; wherefore He found those heathen people, who by the time that was gone, had been out of God's faith and of His love and of His service. They had not been idle in order to do the devil's work; but therefore says the Gospel who had been idle because they had not believed in one God Almighty, nor loved Him, nor served Him. For all that is in the world that is man unless

he loves God Almighty and serves Him, it all may appear
to him lost and idleness. Then Our Lord called the pagans
with His apostles, wherefore they had been idle so long,
because they had not been in His service. Then the pagans
answered that no one had hired them, that is to say, that
they had never had prophets, nor apostles, nor preachers
who showed them, nor taught them how they should believe
in God, nor serve Him. "Go," He said, Our Lord, "into My
vineyard, that is, into My faith and I shall give you your
penny, that is Heavenly bliss." Then heathen men went by
the dawn into Christ's service. And we that are come from
them and have received Christianity, are entered into
Christ's service; therefore we shall have our penny, that is,
the bliss of Heaven all as well as they who came in the
morning. For we hope also in order to have heavenly bliss
as the patriarchs and the prophets and the apostles and the
good men who served Almighty God while in this world.

So as we have said of different ages that Almighty God
put workmen into His vineyard, as we might say, of the
age of every man. For Almighty God puts workmen into
His vineyard in the morning when He calls of such there be
in His service in their childhood, when they go from this
world so that they are not in deadly sin. In the morning
hours, He sends men into His vineyard whom He turned
into His service at the age of [a young] man. At midday
when the day is all the hottest betokens those men of thirty
winters or of forty for the nature of man is of greater
strength and of greater heat in those years. So evening betokens the old age of man that is the end of his life. Our
Lord puts workmen into His vineyard against the evening
when many in old age go out from their sins into Christ's
service. Also shall they have the bliss of Heaven as those
who come first into the vineyard. Therefore for this great
bounty that Our Lord gives, not sells, no man [should]

delay in order to go to Almighty God or to serve Him; for also say the Holy Scriptures that no one knows the day of his death, for often man may hope for a long life and often by deceit is false to himself.

Now, good men, you have heard the Gospel and the example. Now look if ye be within the vineyard, that is, if you are in God's service, if you are without deadly sins, if you hate what He hates, if you love what He loves, and do what He commands; and unless you do, you are out of His vineyard, that is, out of His service. And do ye what Our Lord commands, so you merit the penny, that is, heavenly bliss, you merit that good that no heart may think of, that no ear [may] hear, no tongue [may] tell, the bliss that God keeps for all those who love Him. Thither, Lord, grant us to come. Quod ipse prestare dignetur per etc.

THE AYENBITE OF INWIT,
OR REMORSE OF CONSCIENCE

In Order To Learn To Die

Who has not learned, dies with difficulty. Learn [how] to die, then you shall know [how] to live; for who has not learned to die, shall not know [how] to live well, and the same rightly are called wretched who know not [how] to live nor dare to die. If you will live nobly, learn to die gladly. If you tell me how men shall learn it, I will tell it to you in haste. You shall know that this life is nothing, except death, for death is a going and that each knows; and therefore men say of a man when he [is] dying, "He [is] going," and when he is dead, "He is gone." This life also is nothing except a going forsooth, forsooth a going very short; for all that life of any man though he live a thousand years that shall not be [anything] except a single prick to the sight of the other life that shall last forever without end, either in sorrow or in bliss without end. This we witness well of the King, the earl, the prince, the emperor who had sometimes happiness in this world, but now weeps in Hell, and cries out, yells and grieves, "Ah, alas, what is our worth, our power, honor, nobleness, richness, happiness and boast? All of it is gone more rapidly than a shadow or a bird flying, or a square bolt of a crossbow. And thus goes all our life. Now we were born and in haste die; and all our life is nothing except a little prick, now we are in sorrow without end. Our happiness is gone into weeping, our song into sorrow; garlands robes, playings, eating together and all goods have failed us." Such are the songs of Hell as the Scriptures tell us, in order to show [us] that this life is nothing except a going very short; and this world is nothing except a going and living is nothing except a going. Then is life nothing except death, and that is true as the paternoster; for when you begin to live, in haste you begin to die; and [of] all thy years and all thy time, that is gone, [it is] death which has won and held. You say that you have sixty years, death has these, and nevermore will yield them to thee. Therefore is that wit of the world folly and the clerk, looking for [it,] saw nothing; day and night makes one thing and the more that it makes, the less you know; always dying and they know not [how] to die, for day and night you die as I have told you.

Yet afterwards in other ways, I [shall] teach you this learning so that you know [how] to live well and [how] to die well. Now hear and understand. Death is nothing but a separation of the soul and of the body and that each well knows. Now the wise Cato teaches us: "Learn we," he says, "to die; we [must] separate the soul from the body often." That did the most wise of these philosophers [say] that this life you must hate, and the world you must disdain, and you must not desire a deadly life that they knew by their pleasure; but it is not worth anything to them for they have not grace, nor faith in Jesus Christ. But the holy men who love God and believe that, of three deaths, the two have passed. For there is death from sin and death from the world; now remains the third death, that is, the separation of soul from the body. Between them and Paradise is nothing except a little wall so that they are at fault by thinking and by wishing. And if the body is of this side, the heart and the spirit is of the other side. There they have their existence, as says Saint Paul, their solace, their happiness, their comfort, and all their pleasures. And therefore they hate this life that is nothing but death, and desire their death bodily; for that is the damsel Berebliss that is the death that crowns and puts into bliss all of the saints. Death is to good men the end of all evil and the gate and entrance to all good. Death is the stream that separates death and life. Death is of this side, life of the other side. But the wise of this world who of this half of the stream see so bright, of the other half they see nothing, and therefore they call the writing foolish and blind; for this death they call life, and the death that is to the good the beginning, they call it the end. And therefore they hate death so much for they know not what it is, nor has anything of the other side of the stream remained, nor know what goes out.

Then if you will know what is good and what is evil, go out of thyself, go out of the world, learn to die. Separate thy soul from thy body by thought; send thy soul into the other world, that is, into Heaven, into Hell, into Purgatory, where you shall see what is good and what is evil. In Hell, you shall see more sorrow than men might devise; in Purgatory, more torments than men might suffer; in Paradise, more happiness than men might desire. Hell shall teach you how God avenges deadly sin; Purgatory shall show you how God cleanses venial sin; in Heaven you shall see openly how virtues and good deeds are recompensed highly. In these three things is all that is needed to know well how men shall know to live and to die well. Now look afterwards a little and weary not yourself with these three things, on account of that you learn to hate sin. Forget thy body once a day; go into Hell into thy living so that you go not into thy dying. This often does the holy man and wise. There you shall see all that the heart hates and avoids, and lack of all good, enough of all evil, fire burning, sulphur stinking, tempest resounding harshly, foul devils, hunger and thirst that men may not cause to cease, different pains and weepings, and sorrows more than the heart might think, or tongue tell, and shall last ever without end. And therefore is the same sorrow well called death without end. And when you see that it profits so dearly to atone for a single deadly sin, you would rather let yourself be flayed quickly than you dare to consent to one single deadly sin.

Afterwards go you into Purgatory where you shall see the pains of the souls that here had repented, but were not fully cleansed. Now they do there the remainder of their penance until that they are bright and clean as they were at the place and at the time when they came out from the baptismal font. But the same penance is very horrible and hard; for all that the holy martyrs ever suffered or wives that labor with child, of sorrow [all this] is nothing but a bath in cold water in respect to the furnace wherein burn the souls until they are cleansed as gold all cleansed in the fire. Men find nothing less than cleansed, for that fire is of such a nature, all that it finds in the soul of guilt, of deed, of speech, of thought, that yearned to sin, either little or much, all is burnt out and cleansed. And there are punished and avenged all venial sins that we call little sins, that we often do, and small foolish thoughts, idle words, nonsense, scorns and all other idleness, until they are worthy to go into Heaven where nothing goes in except it be rightly bright. That same fire dread those who by their might keep them from deadly sins and keep holy their hearts and their bodies and their mouths, and the five senses from all sin; and so live as they should each day to come towards God for judgment. And who therefore may not live without sin; for as Solomon said, "Seven times a day falls a good man." And therefore by holy confession and by tears and by prayers, they do with their might to raise themselves and

to amend; and so judge themselves that they understand
to follow the last judgment, for who truly judges himself
here, [there] is no care for him to be lost on Judgment Day.
And thus men learn to know and to avoid evil, and to hate
all sins, great and small, and to understand the holy dread
of God that is the beginning of a good life and of all good.

But it is not enough to stop the evil except one learns
to do that good and unless one seeks the virtues, for without them no one believes well aright. Then if you will learn
to live well by virtue, learn so, as I have told you, to die.
Separate thy soul from thy body by thought and desire; go
out of this world's dying; go into the land of the living
where none die, nor grow old, that is, in Paradise. There
men learn to live well in wit and courtesy, for there may not
go in any villainy; there is the blissful company of God and
of angels and of the saints; there increases all goods, beauty,
richness, worship, happiness, virtue, love, wit, joy, without
end; there is no hypocrisy, no trouble, no flattery, no discord, no envy, no hunger, no thirst, no heat, no chill, no
evil, no sorrow, no dread of fiends, but always feasts and
Kings' bridal feasts, youth and happiness without end. The
same happiness is so great that who that had taken thereof a
single drop of the least thing that is there, he should be
from the love of God so drunk that all the happiness of this
world should be for him fear and woe; richness, dung;
honor, foulness; and the like. For the great love that he
should have to come there, he should, by a hundred
thousand times, more hardily, hate sin and love virtues
that are all the fear of Hell whereof I have spoken before;
for love is more stronger than dread. And then is that life
fair and honest when men avoid evil, and men do that
good, not for fear of being destroyed but for the desire for
Heaven and for love of God and for the great cleanness

that virtue and the good life have. And the same that love leads, he seeks quicker and expends himself less than he who serves God by fear. The hare yearns [to run,] the greyhound follows him; the one by fear, the other by desire; the one flies, the other drives him. The holy men yearn as the greyhound, who all day have their eyes to Heaven where they see the prey that they drive; and therefore they forget all other goods as does the gentle hound when he cares for his prey before his eyes.

This is that life of the well loving of gentle heart and subdued that love virtue so much and hate sin so that if they were sure that men should not know it, nor God avenge it, they deign not to sin; but all their thinking and all their desires look and prepare with their clean hearts that they be worthy to have bliss of Paradise, where no churl shall come in, nor false one, nor thief, nor proud one, for the worse should be the company.

TREVISA'S TRANSLATION
OF HIGDEN'S POLYCHRONICON

Book I, Chapter LVIII
The Inhabitants of Britain

Britains lived first in this land, the year of Eli, the priest eighteen; of Silvius Posthumus, King of the Latins, eleven; after the taking of Troy, three and forty years; before the building of Rome, four hundred and two and thirty [years.] They came hither and took their course from Amorica that is now the other Britain; they held for a long time in the southern part of the country of this land. It befell afterwards in the time of Vespasian, Duke of Rome, that the Picts out of Scythia sailed into the ocean and driven about by the winds and entered into the northern coast of Ireland and found there Scots and entreatied in order to have a place to live in and might not obtain; for Ireland, as the Scots said, might not sustain both people. The Scots sent the Picts to the north side of Britain and promised them help against the Britains, who were enemies, if they should arise, and took them to wives from their daughters upon such conditions: if doubtful who should have the right in order to be King, they should rather choose themselves a King from the mother's side than from the father's side, of the women kin rather than from the men kin. In the time of Vespasian, the emperor, when Marius Arviragus, his son was King of Britain; one Roderich, King of the Picts, came out of Scythia and began to destroy Scotland. Then Marius the King, slew this Roderich and gave the north part of Scotland which was called Caithness, to the men who were come with Roderich and were overcome by him, in order to live in. But these men had no wives and might not have any from the nation of Britain; therefore they sailed into Ireland and took them to wives the daughters of Irishmen with this agreement that the mother's blood should be put before in succession of heritage. Nevertheless, Servius, after Virgil, said that the Picts were Agatirses who had some dwelling places about the water of Scythia and they were called Picts because of the painting and smearing of wounds that are seen on their bodies; for they had much slimy matter in [their] throats and had often boisterously let blood and had many wounds seen on their bodies so that they seemed as they were men painted with wounds; therefore they were called Picts as they were painted men. These men and the Goths are as one people; for when Maximus, the tyrant was gone out of Britain into France in order to occupy the empire, then Gratianus and Valentinianus who were brothers and friends of the emperor, brought these Goths out of Scythia with great gifts, with flattery and fair promises into the north country of Britain, for they were stalwart and strong men of arms and sent them by ship to war upon the Britains who were then naked and bare without knights and men of arms. And so thieves and rascals were made men of land and of the country and lived in the north country and built there cities and towns. Carausius, the tyrant, slew Bassianus with the help and treason of the Picts who came in help and succor of Bassianus and gave the Picts a living place in Albania which is Scotland. There they lived a long time afterwards [and] mixed with the Britains. Then afterwards these Picts quickly occupied the north side of Scotland, it seems that the living place that Carausius gave them is the South side of Scotland that stretches from the crossing wall of Roman work to the Scottish Sea and includes Galway and Lodovia, Lodway. Thereof, Bede, Book Three, Second Chapter, speaks in this way: Ninian, the holy man, converted the South Picts; afterwards the Saxons came and made that country belong to Bernicia, the north part of Northumberland, until that Cynadius, the son of Alpinus, King of Scotland, put out the Picts and made that country that is between the Tweed River and the Scottish Sea, belong to his kingdom. Afterwards, a long time, the Scots were led by Duke Reuda and came out of Ireland that is the proper country of the Scots, and with love or with strength, made them a place fast by the Picts, in the north side of the arm of the sea that breaks into land on the west side that separated in old times, the Britains and the Picts. From this Duke Reuda, the Scots had the name, and were called Dalreudines as part of it is Reuda, for in their speech a part is called "dal." The Picts might have no wives from the Britains, but they took themselves wives from the Irish-Scotch and cherished them fair in order to live with them and granted them land by the seaside where the sea is narrow; That land is now called Galway. The Irish-Scotch landed at Argyle that is the Scotish cliff, for the Scots landed there in order to harm the Britains, or because that place is next to Ireland in order to come ashore in Britain. And so the Scots, after the Britains and Picts made the third group of people living in Britain.

Then after that came the Saxons, at the entreaty of the Britons to help them against the Scots and Picts. And the Britons were put out anon to Wales and the Saxons occupied the land little by little and afterwards more and more, straight anon to the Scottish Sea; and so the Saxons made the fourth group of people in the land of Britain. For the Saxons and Angles came out of Germany; yet some

Britains who lived near, called them Germans for short. Nevertheless, about the year of Our Lord eight hundred, Egbertus, King of the West Saxons, commanded and ordered all men of that land to be called Englishmen. Then after that the Danes took the land for about two hundred years, that is, in meaning, from the time of the aforementioned Egbertus right until the time of Saint Edward, and made the fifth group of people in the land but they failed afterwards. At the last came the Normans under Duke William and subdued the Englishmen, and yet holds the land; and they made the sixth [group] of people in the land. But in the time of Henry the first came many Flemings and took a living place for a time besides Mailros on the west side of England and made the seventh [group] of people in the land. Nevertheless, by order of the same King, they were transferred thence and put to this side of Haverford, in the west side of Wales. And so now in Britain, Danes and Picts failed completely and five nations live therein; that is, the Scots in Albania that is Scotland; the Britains in Cambria that is Wales, except that the Flemings live in West Wales; and the Normans and Englishmen mingled in all the land. For it is no doubt in stories how and in what manner, the Danes were put away and destroyed out of Britain; now it is to declare how the Picts were destroyed and failed.

Britain was sometimes occupied with the Saxons and peace was made and established with the Picts. Then the Scots that came with the Picts saw that they the Picts were less [in number] than the Scots and were nobler of deeds and better men at arms than were the Scots; then the Scots turned to their kind of treason that they used often, for in treason they pass other men and are traitors, as it were, by nature. For they invited to a feast all the greats of the Picts and waited their time when the Picts were at ease and merry and well drunk, and drew out the nails that held up the hollow benches under the Picts, and the Picts suddenly and unaware fell over their hams into a wonderful pitfall. Then the Scots fell on the Picts and slew them and left [them] not alive; and so of the two people the better warriors were wholly destroyed. But the others, that is the Scots, who were indeed different from the Picts, took profit by that false treason; for they took all the land and hold it yet hitherto, and call it Scotland after their own name. That time, that was in the time of King Edgar, Cynadius, son of Alpinus, was the leader of the Scots and warred in the Picts' land and destroyed the Picts; he warred six times against the Saxons and took all the land that is between the Tweed River and the Scottish Sea with wrong and with strength.

Chapter LIX

On The Languages of The Inhabitants

As it is known how many groups of people are in this land, there are also of so many people, languages and tongues; nevertheless, Welshmen and Scotsmen that are not mixed with other peoples, hold well near their first language and speech, except the Scots who were some time confederated to and lived with the Picts draw somewhat after their speech [the Picts.] But the Flemings who live in the west side of Wales have left their strange speech and speak like Saxons indeed. Also Englishmen, though they had from the beginning three manners of speech, southern, northern, and middle speech, in the middle of the land as it came from the three groups of people from Germany; nevertheless, by commingling and mixing, first with the Danes and afterwards with the Normans, in general the language of the country is impaired and some use strange stammering, chattering, snarling, and chatter, gnashing of teeth. This impairment of the mother tongue is because of two things. One is because the children in school against usage and the way of all other nations, are compelled for to leave their own language and for to construe their lessons and their things in French and have since the Normans first came to England. Also the children of gentlemen are taught in order to speak French from the time that they are rocked in their cradles and can speak and play with a child's broach; and rural men would liken themselves to gentlemen and try with great care in order to speak French in order to be thought more of.

This way was much used before the first plague and is since somewhat changed. For John Cornwall, a teacher of grammar, changed the teaching in grammar school and the construction of French into English; and Richard Pencrych learned that manner of teaching from him and other men from Pencrych so that now the year of Our Lord, one thousand, three hundred, four score and five, from King Richard the Second after the conquest nine, in all grammar schools of England, children leave French and construe and learn in English and have thereby an advantage on one side and a disadvantage on another. Their advantage is that they learn their grammar in less time than children were wont to do; the disadvantage is that now children of grammar school know no more French than knows their left heel, and this is harm for them, and should they pass [across] the sea and travel in foreign lands and in many [other] circumstances too. Also gentlemen have now much left in order to teach their children French.

It seems a great wonder how English that is the mother tongue of Englishmen and their own language and tongue, is so different of sound in this land; and the language of

Normandy is a new comer from another land and has one manner of sound among all men that speak it aright in England. Nevertheless, there is as many different ways of French in the realm of France, as is different ways of English in the realm of England. Also, of the aforesaid Saxon tongue, that is divided in three and is scarcely remained with few rural men and [it] is a great wonder; for men of the east with men of the west, as it was, under the same part of heaven, agree more in the sounding of speech than men of the north with the men from the south. Therefore, it is that the Mercians who are men of the middle of England, as it were partners of the ends, understand better the side languages, northern and southern, than the northerners and southerners understand each other. All the language of the Northumbrians, and especially at York, is so sharp, slittering and harsh sounding and unpleasant that we southern men scarcely understand that language. I believe that this is because that they are near to foreign men and aliens who speak strangely and also because that the kings of England always lived far from that country; for they are more turned to the south country, and if they go to the north country, they go with great help and strength. The cause why they are more in the south country than in the north, may be better corn land, more people, more noble cities, and more profitable harbors.

THE ENGLISH PROCLAMATION OF
HENRY THIRD

Henry, through God's grace, King of England, Lord of Ireland, Duke of Normandy, of Aquitaine and Earl of Anjou, sends greetings to all his faithful, learned and lay, in Huntingdonshire; that know ye well all that we will and favor that all our counsellors or the greater part of them that are chosen through us and through the people of the land in our kingdom, have done and shall do in the honor of God and in our truth, for the profit of the land, through provisions of the aforesaid counsellors, be steadfast and enduring in all things without end. And we command all our true [subjects] in the faith that they owe us that they steadfastly hold and swear to hold and to defend the statutes that are made and are to make through the aforesaid counsellors or through the greater part of them just as it is said before; and that each help the other in that in order to act by the same oath against all men rightly for to act and to seize. And none take from the land or from the property wherethrough this provision might be hindered or made worse in any way. And if any come here against any other, we will and command that all our true [subjects] hold them deadly foes. And because we desire that this be steadfast and lasting, we send you this writ openly, sealed with our seal to hold among you in hoard. Witnessed by ourselves at London, this eighteenth day of the month of October in the two and fortieth year of our crowning. And this was done before our sworn counsellors: Boniface, Archbishop of Canterbury; Walter of Cantelupe, Bishop of Worcester; Simon of Montfort, Earl in Leicester; Richard of Clare, Earl in Gloucester and in Hertford; Roger Bigod, Earl in Norfolk and Marshall in England; Pierce of Savoy; William De Fors, Earl in Albemarle; John of Plessis, Earl in Warwick; John Geoffrey's son, Peter of Montfort; Richard of Grey; Roger of Mortimer; James of Aldithley; and before others enough.

And in the same words is sent into every other shire over all the kingdom in England and also into Ireland.

ADAM DAVY'S DREAMS
ABOUT EDWARD II

To Our Lord Jesus Christ in Heaven,
I today show my dream,
That I dreamed in one night
Of a knight with much might;
His name is called Sir Edward, the King,
Prince of Wales, of England the fair thing.
I dreamed that he was well armed
Both with iron and with steel,
And on his helmet that was of steel
A crown of gold became him well.
Before the shrine of Saint Edward he stood,
With happy face and mild of mood,
With two knights armed on either side
So that he might neither go nor ride.
Hatefully they laid upon him
As they might do with swords.
He stood there very very still,
And suffered all together their will;
No stroke gave he backward
To those who were against him.
Wounds were there bloody none,
For all that was there done to him.
After that I thought immediately,
As the two knights were gone,
In either ear of our King,
There sprang out a very fair thing.
They grew out as bright as the gleams
That shine from the sunbeams.

Of different colors were they
That came out of both his ears;
Four ribbons all in a row from either ear
Of different colors, red and white were they;
As far as I thought that I might see
They spread far and wide in the country
Forsooth, I dreamed this same dream—
I take to witness God of Heaven—
The Wednesday before the beheading of Saint John,
It is more than twelve months ago.
God grant me such heavenly bliss,
As I dreamed in this dream as it is.
Now God who is the Heavenly King
To much joy turn this dream.

 Another dream I dreamed on a Tuesday night,
Before the feast of All Hallows, of that same knight,
His name is named here before;—
Bless be the time that he was born;
For we shall see the day,
He be chosen Emperor of Christianity.
God grant us the same favor,
That these tidings we soon hear
Of Sir Edward, our precious King.
I dreamed of him another fair dream;
To Our Lord of Heaven, I tell this,
That my dream turn to much happiness.
I thought he rode upon an ass,
And that I take God to witness;
He was wrapped in a gray mantle;
Towards Rome he took his way.
Upon his head sat a gray cap,
It seemed very suitable for him.
He rode without hose and shoe,
His custom was not for to do so;

His legs seemed all blood-red;
My heart wept for great fear.
As a pilgrim he rode to Rome,
And thither he came very quickly.
  The third dream I dreamed one night
Of that same precious knight
The Wednesday at night it was
Next to the day of Saint Lucy before Christmas.
I show this, to God of Heaven,
To much joy turn He my dream.
I thought that I was at Rome
And thither I came very soon;
The Pope and Sir Edward, our King,
They both had a new dubbing.
A gray cap was his clothing;
Of other clothing I saw nothing.
The Pope went before, mitered well fair enough,
The King, Edward, came crowned with great happiness;
That betokens that he shall be
Emperor in Christianity.
Jesus Christ, full of grace,
Grant our King in every place
Mastery over his enemies,
And over all wicked Saracens.
  I dreamed a dream on the feast of the Purification,
Of that same precious knight;
God I show it to and take to witness,
And so shield me from sin and guilt.
Into the chapel I came by our Lady;
Jesus Christ, her dear Son, stood by;
On the cross He was a lovely man
As such who was put on the cross.
He unnailed His two hands,
And said He would go with the knight;

"Maiden and mother and mild Queen,
Might I see that knight today.
Dear Mother, give me leave,
For I may no longer remain;
I must convey to that same knight
That has served us day and night,
On a pilgrimage he will go
To be avenged of our foes."
"Dear Son, Your will, so it must be,
For that knight has both night and day served me,
According to both Our will, very fair certainly,
Therefore he has served the bliss of the Heavenly king-
    dom."
God who is in Heaven so bright
Be with our King both day and night.
Amen, Amen, so might it be;
Thereto pray a "paternoster" and an "ave."
  Adam the marshall of Stratford-atte-Bowe,
Indeed, very well widely is his name known,
He himself dreamed these dreams,
To witness he takes Jesus, the Heavenly King;
On Wednesday in the clean spring,
A voice bid me I should not faint;
Of the dreams that here are written,
I should quickly let my lord, King know.
I answered that I might not go because of the dark.
The voice bade me go, for light I should not fail,
And that I should stop for nothing,
That I should show my King my dream.
Therefore I went very quickly,
Eastward as I thought I must go;
The light of Heaven came to me,
As I should go on my way.
Lord, my body I give unto Thee,

What Your will is to do with me.
I take to witness God of Heaven,
That truly I dreamed this same dream;
I care not what You do with my body,
As certainly Jesus of Heaven takes care of my soul.
   The Thursday next after the Burying of Our Lady,
I thought an angel came by Sir Edward;
The angel took Sir Edward by the hand,
All bleeding as were the four front claws of the Lamb.
At Canterbury, before the high altar, the King stood,
Clothed all in dark red; he was of that complexion, red
    as blood.
God who was put on the cross on Good Friday,
So turn my dreaming, night and day, to much good.
Two points there are that are hidden
For [it] is not for me [to show] to learned or unlearned;
But to Sir Edward, our King,
To him will I show this dream.
I tell you truly without lies,
As God of Heaven chose the maid Mary to mother,
The angel came to me, Adam Davy and said,
"Except you, Adam, show this, a very evil reward is for
    thee."
I show you this same dream,
As the angel showed it to me in a vision;
Except this sign happens, put me in prison.
Lord, my body is to Your will;
Though You will therefore destroy,
I will take it in patience,
As God grants us Heavenly bliss;
And let us never thereof miss,
That we might not go there in cleanness.
Amen, Amen, so might it be,
And let us never in another way go.

Whosoever will speak with me, Adam, the marshall,
In Stratford-atte-Bowe, he is known and above all;
I show this, not in order to have a reward
But for fear of Almighty God,
For it is true.

THE FIRST PETITION TO PARLIAMENT IN ENGLISH

To the most noble and worthiest Lords, most rightful and wisest Counsel to our liege Lord, the King; complain, if it please you, the people of the Mercery of London, as a member of this same city, of many subtle wrongs and also open oppressions done to them for a long time here before passed. Of which one was where the election of mayoralty is to be to the freemen of the city, with good and peaceable advice of the wisest and truest, on one day in the year freely,—there, notwithstanding, the same freedom and franchise, Nicholas Brember, with his supporters, proposed him, the year next after John Northampton, mayor of the same city, with strong hands, as it is full known, and through debate and stronger party against the peace, before provided; was chosen mayor, in destruction of many rights. For in the same year, the aforesaid Nicholas, without need, against the peace, made different armings by day and also by night and destroyed the King's true faithful; some by open slaughter, some by false imprisonments, and some fled the city for fear, as it is openly known.

And so furthermore in order to sustain these wrongs and many others, the next year after, the same Nicholas, against the aforesaid freedom and true commons, did cry openly that no man should come to choose their mayor except such as were summoned, and those who were summoned were of his arrangement and after his advice. And in the night, next after following, he did carry great quantity of arms to the guildhall, with which, as well strangers from the country as others from within, were armed in the morning against his own proclamation, that was, such that no man should be armed; and certain ambushes were laid that when freemen of the city came to choose their mayor, armed [men] broke upon [them,] crying with a loud voice, "Slay, slay," following them; wherethrough the people for fear fled to [the] houses and other hidings, as in a land of war, frightened to be dead together.

And thus yet hitherward has the mayoralty been held as it were by conquest or dominion, and many other offices also, so that what a man, privately or openly especially, that he might know wrong, complained, or held against any of his wrongs, or by putting forth of whomso it were, were it never so improper, were impeached and were it displeasing to him, Nicholas, immediately was imprisoned, and though it was against the falsehood of the least officer that was pleasing for him [Nicholas] to maintain, was held untrue liegeman to our King; for who reproved such an officer, maintained by him, of wrong or else, he forfeited against him Nicholas, and he, unworthy as he said, represented the King's estate. Also if any man because of service or other faithful engagement, approached a lord, to which lord, he, Nicholas, feared his falsehood to be known to, anon was impeached that he was false to the Counsel of the city, and so to the King.

And if in general his falseness were denied, as from us together from the Mercery or other crafts, or any counsel would have taken to stand against it, or—as time out of mind has been used—would meet together [to decide] how lawful as it were for our need or profit, we were immediately impeached for revolters against the peace and falsely many of us for that yet stand indicted. And we are openly disgraced, held untrue and traitors to the King; for the same Nicholas said before the mayor, aldermen, and before our craft gathered in the place of record, that twenty or thirty of us were worthy to be drawn and hanged, which thing please your worthy lordship by a just judge to be proved or disproved the whether that truth may show; for truth among us of few, or else no man, many days, dare be showed; and not only unshowed or hidden has it been by man now, but also from the time before the most profitable points of true government of the city, compiled together by the long labor of discrete and wise men, without counsel of true men—for they should not be known, nor continued —in the time of Nicholas Exton, mayor, were burnt utterly.

And so far forth, falsehood has been used so that often times, he, Nicholas Brember, said in sustaining his falsehood, our liege lord's will was such that never was such, as we suppose. He said, when he had slandered us, which of us would yield him false to his King, the King should do him favor, cherish him, and be a good Lord to him; and if any of us all, that with God's help have and should endeavor to be true, was so bold to proffer the proving himself true; immediately was ordered to prison as well by the mayor that is now, as by him, Nicholas Brember, before.

Also we have been commanded ofttimes, upon our allegiance, to unneedful and unfaithful diverse doings, and also to withdraw ourselves by the same order from things needful and lawful, as was shown when a company of good women, where men dared not, went barefooted to our liege Lord to seek favor from him for the true men as they supposed; for then were such proclamations made that no man or woman should approach our liege Lord for seeking his favor, and very many other orders also, before and after, by suggestion and information, so that the condition of their falseness would not be known to our liege Lord. And lords, by your leave, our liege Lord's order to simple and unknowing men is a great thing to be used so familiarly without need; for they, unwise to observe it, might lightly forfeit [their rights] there again.

Therefore, gracious Lords, please it to you to take heed in what manner and where our liege Lord's power has been misused by the aforesaid Nicholas and his supporters, for since these wrongs beforesaid have been used as accidental or common branches outwardly, it shows well the root of them is a ragged subject or stem inward, that is, the aforesaid briar or Brember, the which uses common wrongs, and many other, if it please you, must be showed and well known by an indifferent judge and mayor of our city; the which by your rightful Lordship, granted foremost principal remedy, as God's law and all reason would, that no judge stand together judge and party, wrongs should be more openly known and truth dare appear. And else, as among us, we cannot know in what manner, without a much greater trouble, since the government of this city stands as it is beforesaid, and stands well while victualers, by sufferance, presume this state upon them; the which government before this time hidden to many people, shows itself now openly, whether it has been a cause or beginning of division in the city, and after, in the realm, or no. . . .

Wherefore for greater need, as to you most worthy, most rightful and wisest Lords and Counsel, to your liege Lord, the King, we beseech meekly for your favor [for] the correction of all the beforesaid wrongs, and that it please your lordship to be gracious intermediaries to your liege Lord, the King, that such wrongs be known to him and that we might show ourselves and after be held so true to him as we are and ought to be. Also we beseech unto your gracious lordship that if any of us, in particular or in general, be impeached to your liege Lord or to his worthy Counsel, by coming with others or approaching to your King, as with

Brember or his abettors, with any wrong witness-bearing, as that it stood otherwise among us here than as it is now proved it has stood, or any other wrong suggestion of which your liege Lord has been unlawfully informed, that then your worshipful lordship be such that we might come in answer to excuse ourselves; for we know well, as in respect to much the more part of us and as, we hope, for all, all such wrongs have been unintentional to us, or else entirely against your will.

And rightful lords, for one of the greatest remedies with others in order to stand against many of these aforesaid troubles among us, we pray with meekness, this especially, that the statute ordained and made by parliament, held in Westminster, in the sixth year of our King, now reigning, might stand in strength and be executed as well here in London as elsewhere in the realm, the which is this:

Item ordinatum est et statutum, quod nec in civitate Londonie nec in aliis civitatibus, burgis, villis, vel portubus maris, per totum regnum predictum, aliquis vitallarius officium judicale de cetero habeat, exerceat, neque occupet quovis modo, nisi in villis ubi alia persona sufficiens ad hujus statum habendus repperiri non poterit, dumtamen idem judex pro tempore quo in officio illo steterit ab exercicio vitallarii, sub pena forisfacture victualium suorum sic venditorum, penitus cesset et se abstineat, per se et suos omino ab eodem, et cet.

THE PARDONER'S TALE

FROM

CHAUCER'S CANTERBURY TALES

In Flanders, one time, was a company
Of young people that practiced folly,
As riot, gambling, brothels, taverns,
Whereas with harps, lutes and guitars
They danced and played at dice both day and night,
And ate also and drank over their might;
Through which they did the devil's sacrifice
Within that devil temple in a cursed wise
By superfluities abominable.
Their oaths were so great and so damnable
That it is horrible for to hear them swear,
Our blessed Lord's body they to pieces tear;
They thought the Jews had torn Him not enough,
And each of them at the other's sins laughed.
And right anon then came female dancers
Shapely and small, and young female fruit-sellers,
Singers with harps, bawds, confectioners,
Which were the very devil's officers,
To enkindle and blow the fire of lechery,
That is tied unto gluttony.
The Holy Writ take I to my witness,
That luxury is in wine and drunkenness.
Lo, how that drunken Lot unkindly
Lay by his daughters two unwittingly.
So drunk he was he knew not what he wrought.
Herod, who the stories so well sought,
When he was filled of wine at his feast,
Right at his own table, he gave his behest

To slay John the Baptist fully guiltless.
Seneca said a good word doubtlessly;
He said he can no difference find
Between a man who is out of his mind
And a man which that is drunken,
Except that madness in a shrew fallen
Perserveres longer than does drunkenness.
    Oh, gluttony, full of cursedness;
Oh, first cause of our confusion,
Oh, the origin of our damnation,
Until Christ had bought us with His blood again!
Lo, how dear, shortly for to say,
Paid for was this cursed villainy;
Corrupt was all this world because of gluttony.
Adam, our father, and his wife also,
From Paradise to labor and to woe
Were driven for this vice, it is no dread;
For while that Adam fasted as I read,
He was in Paradise and when that he
Ate of the forbidden fruit of the tree,
Anon he was outcast to woe and pain.
Oh, gluttony, of thee well ought we to complain!
    These rioters three of which I tell,
Long before prime was rung from any bell,
Had set themselves in a tavern to drink;
And as they sat they heard a bell clink
Before a corpse was carried to his grave.
So that one of them began to call to his knave,
"Go quickly," quote he, "and ask readily
What corpse is this that passes here nearby
And see that you report his name well."
"Sir," quote this boy, "it is not necessary at all,
It was told to me before you came here two hours;

He was, pardee, an old fellow of yours,
And suddenly he was slain tonight,
Very drunk, as he sat on his bench upright.
There came a private thief, men call Death,
That in this country all the people slay,
And with his spear, he smote his heart in two
And went his way without words more.
He has a thousand slain in this pestilence,
And, master, before you come into his presence,
I think that it is necessary
For to be aware of such an adversary;
Be ready in order to meet him evermore
Thus taught me my dame, I say no more."
"By Saint Mary," said this taverner,
"The child tells the truth for he has slain this year,
Hence over a mile within, a great village,
Both man and woman, child and servant and page;
I believe his habitation be there.
To be advised great wisdom it were,
Before that he did a man a dishonor."

    "Yea, by God's arms," quote this rioter,
"It is such peril with him for to meet?
I shall seek him by way and by street,
I make promise to God's worthy bones!
Hearken, fellows, we three are all one,
Let each of us hold up his hand to the other
And each of us become the other's brother,
And we will slay this false traitor Death.
He shall be dead who that so many slays,
By God's dignity, before it be night."

    Together had these three their troth plighted
To live and die each of them for the other,
As though he was his own born brother.

And up they stirred, all drunken in a rage,
And forth they went towards that village
Of which the taverner had spoken before;
And many a horrible oath then had they sworn,
And Christ's blessed body they tore,—
Death shall be dead if that they might catch him.
   When they had gone not fully half a mile,
Right as they would have trodden over a stile,
An old man and a poor [one] met with them.
This old man full meekly greeted them
And said thus, "Now, lords, God see you."
The proudest of these rioters three
Answered back, "What, churl, with sorry grace
Why are you all wrapped up except your face?
Why live you so long, to such a great age?"
   This old man began to look into his visage
And said thus, "For I can not find
A man, though that I walk to India,
Neither in city nor in any village,
That would change his youth for my age;
And therefore must I have my age still
As long a time as it is God's will.
Death, alas, would not have my life;
Thus walk I like a restless caitiff,
And on the ground which is my mother's gate,
I knock with my staff both early and late,
And say, 'Dear mother, let me in.
Lo, how I vanish, flesh and blood and skin;
Alas, when shall my bones be at rest?
Mother, with you would I change my strife
That in my chamber, a long time has been,
Yea, for a higher cloth to wrap myself.'
But yet for me she would not do this favor;
For which full pale and withered is my face.

But, sirs, to you it is no courtesy
To speak to an old man [of] villainy,
Except he trespasses in word or else in deed.
In Holy Writ you may yourself well read,
Against an old man, hoar upon his head,
You should arise; wherefore I give you advice,
No one does to an old man harm now,
No more than that you would men do to you
In age, if that you live so long;
And God be with you where you go or ride,—
I must go thither as I have to go."
    "Nay, old churl, by God thou shall not so,"
Said the other gambler anon;
"Thou depart not so lightly, by Saint John!
Thou spoke right now of this traitor Death,
Who in this country all our friends slay;
Have here my truth, as thou are his spy,
Tell where he is or thou shall pay for it,
By God and the holy sacrament.
For truly thou are one of his assent
To slay us young people, thou false thief."
    "Now, sirs," quote he, "if that you be so lief
To find Death, turn up this crooked way,
For in that grove, I left him, by my faith,
Under a tree and there he will abide;
Because of your boast, he will hide nothing of himself.
See ye that oak? Right there ye shall find him;
God save you who bought again mankind,
And satisfy you." Thus said the old man;
And each of these rioters ran
Until he came to that tree and they found there
Of florins of fine gold, coined round,
Well nigh in eighty bushels, as they thought.
No longer then after Death they sought,

But each of them was so glad of that sight,
For that the florins were so fair and bright,
That down they placed themselves by that precious
  hoard.
The worse of them he spoke the first word.
  "Brethern," quote he, "Take heed what I say,
My wit is great though that I jest and play.
This treasure has fortune given to us
In mirth and jollity our life to live,
And lightly as it comes so will we spend.
Eh, by God's precious dignity, who knew
Today that we should have so fair a favor?
But might this gold be carried from this place
Home to my house or else unto yours,—
For well we know that all this gold is ours,—
Then were we all in high felicity.
But truly by day it may not be;
Men would say that we were thieves strong,
And for our own treasure, do hang us.
This treasure must be carried by night
As wisely and as slyly as it might.
Wherefore I advise that a cut among us all
Be drawn, and let see where the cut will fall;
And he that has the cut with glad heart
Shall run into the town and that very fast,
And bring us bread and wine very privately.
And two of us shall keep subtly
This treasure well, and if he will not tarry,
When it is night, we will this treasure carry
By one assent whereas we think best."
  That one of them the cut brought in his fist,
And bade them draw and see where it would fall;
And it fell to the youngest of them all,
And forth towards the town he went anon.

And all as soon as he was gone,
That one of them spoke thus unto the other;
   "Thou knowest well thou art my sworn brother;
Thy profit will I tell thee anon.
Thou knowest well that our fellow is gone,
And here is gold and that a very great plenty,
That shall be divided among us three;
But, nevertheless, if I can shape it so
That it be divided between us two,
Had I not done a friend's turn for thee?"
   That other answered, "I know not how that may be;
He knows how that gold is with us two;
What shall we do, what shall we to him say?"
   "Shall it be secret?" said the first shrew,
"And I shall tell in words few
What we shall do and bring it well about."
   "I grant," quote the other, "out of doubt,
That, by my faith, I shall not betray thee."
   "Now," quote the first, "thou knowest well we are **two**
And two of us shall be stronger than one.
See, when that he is set, thou right anon
Arise as though thou wouldst with him play,
And I shall tear him through the two sides
While that you struggle with him as in a game,
And with thy dagger look thou do the same;
And then all this gold shall divided be,
My dear friend, between me and thee.
Then may we both our pleasures all fulfill,
And play at dice right at our will."
And thus agreed are these shrews two
To slay the third, as you have heard me say.
   This youngest, which that went into the town,
Very often, in heart, rolls up and down

The beauty of these florins new and bright.
"Oh, Lord," quote he, "if so it be that I might
Have all this treasure to myself alone,
There is no man that lives under the throne
Of God that should live as merry as I."
And at last, the fiend, our enemy,
Put into his thoughts that he should poison buy,
With which he might slay these fellows two;
Because the fiend found him in such living,
That he had let him to sorrow bring,
For this was outwardly his full intent
To slay them both and never to repent.
And forth he goes, no longer would he tarry,
Into the town unto an apothecary,
And asked him that he would sell him
Some poison with which he might his rats kill;
And also there was a polecat in his meadow
That, as he said, had his capons killed;
And fain would he avenge himself, if he might,
On vermin that destroyed him by night.

The apothecary answered, "And thou shall have
A thing that, all, so God my soul save,
In all this world, there is no creature,
That has eaten or drunk of this mixture
Nothing but the amount of a grain of wheat,
That he shall not his life lose anon;
Yes, die he shall in less while
Than thou wilt go apace, not but a mile,
This poison is so strong and violent."

This cursed man has in his hand taken
This poison in a box and after he ran
Into the next street unto a man,
And bought from him large bottles three,

And into the two poison poured he;
The third he kept clean for his drink,
For all the night he shaped himself for to work
In carrying of the gold out from that place.
And when this rioter with sorry grace,
Had filled with wine these great bottles three
To his fellows again returned he.
    What need it to sermonize of it more?
For right as they had planned his death before,
Exactly so they had slain him and that anon.
And when this was done, thus spoke that one:
"Now, let us sit and drink and make us merry,
And afterwards we will his body bury."
And with that word, it happened to him by chance,
To take the bottle where the poison was,
And drank and gave his fellow a drink also;
From which anon they both two died.
But certainly I suppose that Avicenna
Wrote never in any canon, nor in any fen,
More wonderful signs of poisoning
Than had these wretches two before their end.
Thus ended are these homicides two,
And also the false poisoner also.
    Oh, cursed sin of all cursedness!
Oh, traitors to murder, oh, wickedness!
Oh, gluttony, luxury, and gambling!
Thou blasphemer of Christ with villainy
And oaths, great of usage and of pride,—
Alas, mankind—how may it happen
That to thy Creator who that wrought thee,
And with His precious heart's blood bought thee,
Thou art so false and so unkind, alas!
Now, good men, God forgive you your trespasses,
And defend you from the sin of avarice.

NOTES

THE PETERBOROUGH CHRONICLE

Dialect: Northeast Midland
Time: 1132-1154, Middle of Twelfth Century
From: Laud MS. 636 of the Bodleian Library, Oxford,
          (Last of Chronicle from 1080 A.D. to end)
Form: Prose

The Anglo-Saxon Chronicles, of which the Peterborough forms a part, were kept in various monasteries, especially those of Winchester, Canterbury, and Peterborough and are the earliest surviving record of any Western nation written in the native tongue.

Peterborough, in Northampton, the heart of the Midlands, is the location of the Benedictine Abbey of St. Peter which was founded by Oswy, King of Northumbria, and Peada, first Christian King of Mercia, in 655. This monastery, destroyed by the Danes in 870, was re-established in 966 by Athelwold, Bishop of Winchester, who changed the name of the place from Medeshamstede to Peterborough.

* * * *

THE DEDICATION TO THE ORMULUM

Dialect: Northeast Midland
Time: About 1200
From: Junius MS. I of the Bodleian Library, Oxford
Form: Poetry: Long iambic line of fifteen syllables with
          a caesura after the eighth, but without rime or
          regular alliteration

In the Dedication, the author tells us that he was named Orm at baptism and that he is a canon in the Order of St. Augustine. We know no more about him.

This long poem, Ormulum, consists of an introduction, called dedication and preface, paraphrases intended to cover the Gospels read in the Church during the year, and homilies upon them. About one eighth of the intended paraphrases and homilies were completed, or at least remain in manuscript, but what we have extends to nearly ten thousand lines. As a literary work it has little value, but it is especially valuable for the light that it throws on the language of the time. Orm's work looks peculiar even to those who are familiar with Middle English, for he undertook to indicate pronunciation with minute exactness by doubling the consonants and the second elements of short dipthongs, along with occasional use of accents and breves. While it is debatable exactly what he was trying to do, his orthography is of practical value in determining vowel quantity.

> Annd unnc birrþ biddenn Godd tatt he forrzife hemm
>   here sinne;
>
> Annd unnc birrþ boþe lofenn Godd off þatt itt wass
>   bigunnenn,

*   *   *   *

THE BESTIARY

Dialect: Southeast Midland
Time: First half of Thirteenth Century
From: Arundel MS. 292 of the British Museum
Form: Poetry: Some rime but many irregularities

The poem consists of mostly fanciful descriptions of thirteen animals with allegorical interpretations of their imaginary characteristics applied to man in his earthly struggle to gain Heaven.

The first twelve sections are based on the Latin *Physiologus,* of Theobaldus, an Italian monk of the eleventh century, the thirteenth upon Alexander Neckam's *De Naturis Rerum.*

* * * *

THE STORY OF JOSEPH

Dialect: Southern portion of East Midland
Time: First part of Thirteenth Century
From: MS. 444 of Corpus Christi College Library, Cambridge, (MS. of *Genesis and Exodus,* this selection an excerpt)
Form: Poetry: Iambic rimed couplet of four stresses, many syllabic irregularities present

This poem is based mainly on the *Historia Scholastica* of Peter Comester, composed between 1169 and 1175, and freely omits many parts of the Bible story and makes additions of Medieval legend and interpretation.

* * * *

FLORIS AND BLANCHEFLEUR

Dialect: Southeast Midland with many strictly Southern forms present
Time: Middle or Second Quarter of Thirteenth Century
From: MS. Gg. 4, 27, 2 of Cambridge University Library
Form: Poetry: Rimed couplet of four, sometimes three, stresses

The story: Floris and Blanchefleur had become enamored of each other as children. The father of Floris, the King of Spain, disapproves of this union and suggests killing

Blanchefleur. In the original French version Blanchefleur is the daughter of a Christian captive and the father of Floris a Saracen. The queen, mother of Floris, proposes sending him away and Floris goes. Blanchefleur is then sold to the Admiral of Babylon for a marvellous cup, and a tomb is erected. When Floris returns, he is told that Blanchefleur is dead, and becomes so broken-hearted that he tries to commit suicide. His parents become so concerned that they tell him the truth. Floris immediately sets out to recover Blanchefleur and is given a marvellous cup by his father and a magic ring by his mother. He has various adventures along the way and finally comes to Babylon. Here by giving the marvellous cup to the Porter and promising him much more wealth, the Porter agrees to help Floris into the tower. Then follows our selection.

* * * *

THE DEBATE OF THE BODY AND THE SOUL

Dialect: East Midland with more Northern than Southern forms but still a considerable amount of Southern

Time: Second half of Thirteenth Century

From: Laud MS. 108 of the Bodleian Library, Oxford

Form: Poetry: Eight line stanzas, Iambic lines of four stresses, riming abababab

The debate is based on a motif widely used in Western Europe during the Middle Ages. In Old and Middle English, it is called, *An Address of The Soul to The Body*. The dialogue between the two, the body and the soul, belongs to Middle English only.

* * * *

Adam And Eve

Dialect: Southeast Midland
Time: About 1300
From: Auchinleck MS. at Edinburgh
Form: Poetry: Rimed couplet of four stresses, with oc-
casional lines of three stresses and many irregu-
larities

This is an apocryphal story of the fall of man, his re-
pentence and penance and the deaths of Adam and Eve.

The story: Adam, in his last illness, commands Eve to go
with Seth to Paradise where they are to receive a message
from God. On the way, the devil stops them and bites Seth
on the face, and Seth commands him to be gone. Then our
selection begins.

An addition is made in the version represented by the
Trinity MS., in which Seth brings seeds from Paradise and
places them under Adam's tongue on his deathbed. These
seeds later become the Cross-tree, from which comes the
redemption of the human race.

* * * *

Havelok The Dane

Dialect: Northeast Midland
Time: 1300
From: Laud MS. 108 of the Bodleian Library, Oxford
Form: Poetry: Rimed couplet with regular four stresses

The original dialect has been somewhat changed by the
different scribes, which frequently happens to popular
poems and stories, and the complete poem consists of 3001
lines.

The story: An English King, Athelwold, entrusts his
daughter Goldborough to the care of the Earl of Cornwall,

Godrich, when the King is about to die. He charges Godrich to marry her to the fairest and strongest man that he could find and place the government of England in her hands. The Earl, thinking to seize England for his son, imprisons Goldborough in the castle of Dover. Then our selection takes up Havelok's fortunes in his early life and ends with his arrival in England. Havelok helps Grim, the man who saved him, in his trade as a fisherman at Grimsby. When a famine comes, he leaves his foster father, walks to Lincoln and takes service to the Earl of Cornwall's cook. One day, at some games, Havelok shows his great strength, and Godrich decides to marry Goldborough to this supposed menial. At first Havelok rebels but finally marries Goldborough and takes her to Grimsby with him. At night, Goldborough perceives, as Grim's wife had before, a light coming from Havelok's mouth and the royal mark on his shoulder. An angel also tells her of good fortune to come. At the same time, Havelok dreams that he possessed all Denmark and England. They go to Denmark; with many adventures, Havelok becomes King after Godard is defeated and hanged. He invades England, and Godrich is made prisoner and burnt. Havelok and Goldborough are crowned at London, reigning happily for sixty years.

* * * *

Robert Manning's Handlynge Synne

Dialect: Northeast Midland
Time: Early 14th Century
From: Harleian MS. 1701 of the British Museum (edited by Furnivall, 1802)
Form: Poetry: Rimed couplet with four stresses

Robert Manning was born at Brunne or Bourn, near Market Deeping in Lincolnshire about 1260, and tells us in his prologue that he translated this work in 1303 from *Manuel des Pechiez* of William of Waddington.

The work treats of the seven deadly sins, seven sacraments, the twelve requisites of a good confession, and the twelve resulting graces therefrom.

* * * *

THE WEST MIDLAND PROSE PSALTER

Dialect: Pure West Midland
Time: First half of 14th Century
From: Additional MS. 17,376 of the British Museum
Form: Prose

This Psalter is a close though sometimes mistaken rendering of the Latin text, presumably an Italic version of the Scriptures. The numbering of the Psalms are different from those of modern versions, but in this selection the numbers have been made to correspond with our own.

Although the modern versions of the Psalms are so beautiful, movingly elevating and sublime in language, the same warm feelings are not lost even in the plain, simple and homey words of this prose selection.

* * * *

THE EARL OF TOULOUSE

Dialect: Northeast Midland
Time: Middle of 14th Century
From: MS. Cambridge Ff II, 38 of Bodleian Library, Oxford
Form: Poetry: Twelve line stanzas, riming aabccbddbeeb, the first two verses of each triplet have four stresses, the last verse of the triplet generally three
This poem has 1,224 verses.

The story: Earl Barnard made war upon the Emperor Diocletian because he had deprived Barnard of his land. The Earl was successful and among other captives took Sir Trylabas of Turkey, whom he agrees to free if he will obtain for the Earl a sight of the beautiful Empress Beulylon (other names; Beaulyoun, Beaulilion). The agreement is kept with Barnard showing up as a hermit and receives some coin and a ring from the Empress. At this same time, two knights of the court urge themselves upon the Empress but she refuses them. To get revenge, they accuse her of adultery before the Emperor who condemns her to be burnt alive, unless, as suggested in Parliament, some one shall prove her innocence in combat with the two accusing knights. Our selection begins here showing the general favor for the proposal.

*   *   *   *

GUILD OF THE HOLY TRINITY
AND OF
SAINT WILLIAM OF NORWICH

Dialect: East Midland
Time: Last half of 14th Century
From: MS. in Public Record Office, London, Bundle CCCX 116
Form: Prose

The Parliament held in Canterbury in 1388 ordered the guilds to make "Returns," that is, an account of their formation and the statutes under which the guild operated. This "Return" is representative of those from the other existing guilds of that time.

*   *   *   *

John Myrc's
Instructions For Parish Priests

Dialect: West Midland
Time: About 14th Century
From: MS. Cotton Claudius A II in the British Museum
(edited by Peacock, 1868)
Form: Poetry: Rimed couplet

John Myrc was a canon from Lilleshall, Shropshire, who stated that this piece was a translation from Latin although the source is unknown.

* * * *

Prologue To The Cursor Mundi

Dialect: Midland and Northern
Time: About 1300
From: MS. Cotton Vesp. A III of the British Museum
Form: Poetry: Rimed couplet with four stresses

The Cursor Mundi is a poetic history of the Hebrew and Christian world, based on various sources, namely, the Scriptures, the *Historia Scholastica* of Peter Comester, the apocryphal books of the New Testament, and others.

As in most medieval stories, the legendary parts are not only interesting but show the credulity of the Medieval mind.

* * * *

The Death Of Saint Andrew

Dialect: Northern with mixture of Midland forms
Time: Probably last part of 13th Century
(MS. from 14th Century)
From: MS. Harleian 4, 196 of the British Museum
Form: Poetry: Rimed couplet

The legend of Saint Andrew first appeared in an Old English poem called "Andreas" in the eighth century and in a prose version in the tenth century. There are also such legends in Latin and Greek; the Latin version, however, is the source of the English version.

* * * *

TREATISES OF RICHARD ROLLE OF HAMPOLE

Dialect: Northern
Time: First half of 14th Century
From: Thornton MS. A I, 17 in Library of Lincoln
   Cathedral
Form: Prose

Rolle was a prolific writer of both prose and poetry, Latin and English, and his two most important works are *Prick of Conscience* and *Mirror of Life*.

* * * *

A METRICAL HOMILY
THE SIGNS OF THE DOOM

Dialect: Northern
Time: About 1330
From: MS. in Library of the Royal College of Physicians
   and Surgeons at Edinburgh
Form: Poetry: Rimed couplet with four stresses

In the literature of the North, the homily or sermon became very important and consisted of a paraphrase of a Scriptural quotation, a sermon interpreting it, and a tale or legend illustrating the lesson. In the course of time, these homilies, based on the Gospel stories and following the ecclesiastical year beginning with Advent (around the first of December), became very popular. The homily in our

book is based on the Gospel story for the second Sunday of
Advent.

* * * *

The Songs Of Lawrence Minot

Dialect: Northern with some Midland forms
Time: 1333-1352
From: MS. Cotton Galba E IX of the British Museum
Form: Poetry: A variety of different meters showing the
influence of foreign forms in fourteenth century
England

The Songs of Minot of whom we know nothing except
his name are fine examples of the native political lyric which
in this case takes a religious-patriotic view of the victories
of King Edward and shows the animosity of the English for
the Scots, a feeling that Samuel Johnson still proclaimed in
the eighteenth century.

The three Songs in our book are the first three of the
eleven still extant.

* * * *

Barbour's Bruce
The Pursuit Of King Robert

Dialect: Extreme Northern or Scottish English
Time: Last half of 14th Century
From: MS. G 23 in the Library of St. John's College,
Cambridge, (MS. at Edinburgh used for first four
books in W. W. Skeat's edition)
Form: Poetry: Rimed couplet with four stresses

Barbour was Archdeacon of Aberdeen and traveled to
England and France and served in the service of the King
of Scotland.

The *Bruce* which has about 13,500 lines and portrays the events from 1286 to 1335 is a national epic.

Just before our selection begins John of Lorn had tried to track the King down with a hound, and five of Lorn's men had been slain by the King and his foster-brother. As Lorn and his men approach, the King and his foster-brother retreat into a woods nearby.

* * * *

The Poema Morale Or Moral Ode

Dialect: Southern from middle district of the South
Time: 1170
From: Egerton MS. 613 (two versions) at Oxford
         Egerton e
Form: Poetry: Long lines of seven stresses, riming in
         couplets, many irregularities of syllables

It is a rather short poem of 396 lines beginning with a penitential section of 18 lines in the first person, developing into moralizing in general, and finally approaching a sermon in verse.

* * * *

Arthur's Last Battle
From Layamon's Brut

Dialect: Southern of western section
Time: About 1200
From: MS. Cotton Calig. A IX of the British Museum
Form: Poetry: Alliterative line with irregular rime coup-
         let and irregular number of syllables

The *Brut* is a poem of 16,000 long lines, based on the older alliterative line and was written by a priest, Lazamon (later written Lawemon, but mostly, Layamon), the son of Leovenath of Arnley in North Worcestershire.

This poem is a legendary history of Britain from the destruction of Troy (c. 1200 B.C.) to 689 A.D. and was based on Norman Wace's *Roman de Brut* which in turn was based on Geoffrey of Monmouth's *Historia Regum Britanniae.*

Our selection begins with line 13,996.

* * * *

THE LIFE OF SAINT JULIANA

Dialect: Southern (northern section) with Midland
Time: About 1200
From: MS. Royal 17 A 27 of the British Museum
Form: Prose (see below)

It is debatable whether this piece is prose or poetry, and some actually claim that it is really a poem of long alliterative and rhythmical lines. Although in the original the alliterative and rhythmical elements are noticeable, it is still written as prose, however.

Cynewulf wrote a poetical life of Saint Juliana in Old English.

* * * *

THE ANCREN RIWLE, OR RULE OF NUNS

Dialect: Pure Southern
Time: Beginning of 13th Century
From: Morton's edition (1853) based on MS. Cotton Nero A XIV, Titus D XVIII, Cleopatra C VI in the British Museum, with changes from Kolbing's collation
Form: Prose

The *Rule of Nuns* is an interesting treatment of the duties of convent life, prepared for three sisters who became nuns. The author may have been Richard Poor, born in Tarente, southwest Dorset, and later made Bishop of Chichester, Salisbury and Durham.

Written in a plain, simple style with quotations from the Bible, Church Fathers and with allusions to the lives of the saints, this work has an introduction and eight parts: of religious service, of keeping the heart, of monastic life, of temptation, of confession, of penitence, of love, and of domestic matters. Significantly, there are practically no legendary or moral tales.

* * * *

Robert Of Gloucester's Chronicle
How The Normans Came To England

Dialect: Southern
Time: Last part of 13th Century
From: MS. Cotton Caligula A XI of the British Museum
Form: Poetry: Rimed couplet with irregular stresses, lines of seven stresses with caesura after four, but many have only six stresses

The Gloucester Chronicle relates the history of England from the legendary Brutus to 1271 A.D., and contains about 12,000 long lines (a later version, 12,600), and the sources of this poem are Geoffrey of Monmouth, William of Malmesbury, Henry of Huntington and others.

Our selection consists of ll. 7,395-7,513.

* * * *

Old Kentish Sermons

Dialect: Kentish

Time: About 1250
From: Laud MS. 471 of the Bodleian Library, Oxford
Form: Prose

Only five of these sermons are extant and they were translations from the French of Maurice de Sully (d. 1196). Our selection is sermon four and five.

* * * *

THE AYENBITE OF INWIT
OR
REMORSE OF CONSCIENCE

Dialect: Kentish
Time: First half of 14th Century
From: MS. Arundel 57 of the British Museum
Form: Prose

The author gives his name as Dan Michel of Northgate, Kent, and says that he was an Augustinian monk of Canterbury.

La Somme des Vices et des Vertus by Lorens, a Benedictine monk of the 13th century was translated to produce our work which treats of the ten commandments, of the twelve articles of faith, of the seven deadly sins, etc., including occasional illustrative stories, anecdotes and lives of the saints.

* * * *

TREVISA'S TRANSLATION
OF
HIGDEN'S POLYCHRONICON

Dialect: Southern of Gloucestershire
Time: Last half of 14th Century

From: MS. Cotton Tiberius D VII of the British Museum
Form: Prose
See Introduction

* * * *

THE ENGLISH PROCLAMATION OF HENRY THIRD

Dialect: London, mixture of Southern and Midland
Time: October 18, 1258
From: MS. in Public Record Office, London
Form: Prose

This is the earliest Proclamation in English following the Norman Conquest; of course, before 1066, the Proclamations were in English.

This writ was issued in both French and English and reaffirmed the Provisions of Oxford, wrested from the King earlier that same year.

* * * *

ADAM DAVY'S DREAMS ABOUT EDWARD II

Dialect: London, Pure Midland
Time: Beginning of the 14th Century
From: Laud MS. 622 at the Bodleian Library, Oxford
Form: Poetry: Rimed couplet, irregular number of syllables

The *Dreams* have no literary value but are interesting for the language of the capital city that they exhibit.

* * * *

The First Petition
To
Parliament In English

Dialect: London
Time: 1386
From: MS. of Public Record Office, London
Form: Prose

Aside from its linguistic value, it shows the great amount of in-fighting and perfidy in the municipal politics of London of that day.

It is quite evident that the Petition was done by someone who was not very accomplished in the writing of English.

*   *   *   *

The Pardoner's Tale
From
Chaucer's Canterbury Tales

Dialect: London
Time: Last Decade of 14th Century
From: Ellesmere MS. as reprinted by the Chaucer Society
Form: Poetry: Rimed couplet with lines of five stresses

The Pardoner's Tale is probably the greatest tale told by Chaucer in his Canterbury Tales.

Since there is so much information about Chaucer and his writings available, it would be superfluous to put down any more.